Brush Lettering

STEP BY STEP

Brush Lettering

STEP BY STEP

Jim Gray & Bobbie Gray, CDA

NORTH LIGHT BOOKS
Cincinnati, Ohio
www.nlbooks.com

Other fine North Light Books are available from your local bookstore, art supply store or direct from the publisher.

05 04 03 02 01   5 4 3 2 1

Library of Congress Cataloging-in-Publication Data
Gray, Jim
    Brush lettering step by step / Jim Gray and Bobbie Gray.
       p. cm.
    Includes index.
    ISBN 0-89134-961-8 (pbk. : alk. paper)
     1. Lettering--Technique. 2. Calligraphy--Technique. I. Gray, Bobbie.

NK3600 .G795 2001
745.6'1--dc21   00-062843

Editor: Jennifer Long
Production Coordinator: Sara Dumford
Designer: Sandy Kent
Step-by-step photography: Christine Polomsky
Finished project photography: Al Parrish

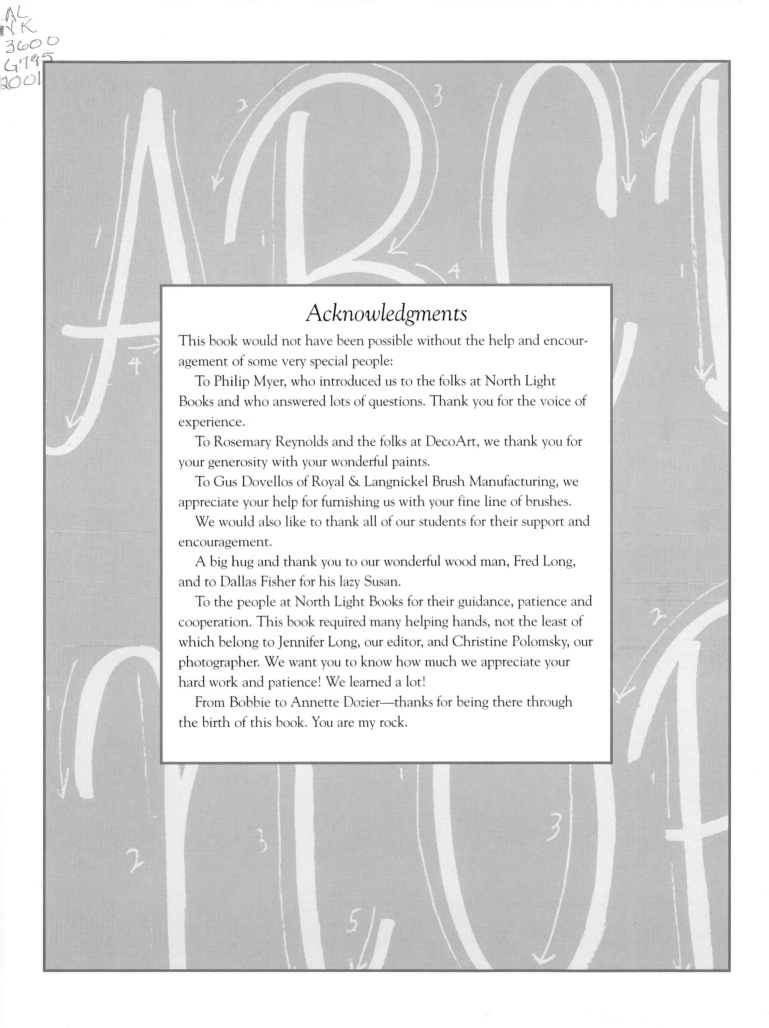

Acknowledgments

This book would not have been possible without the help and encouragement of some very special people:

To Philip Myer, who introduced us to the folks at North Light Books and who answered lots of questions. Thank you for the voice of experience.

To Rosemary Reynolds and the folks at DecoArt, we thank you for your generosity with your wonderful paints.

To Gus Dovellos of Royal & Langnickel Brush Manufacturing, we appreciate your help for furnishing us with your fine line of brushes.

We would also like to thank all of our students for their support and encouragement.

A big hug and thank you to our wonderful wood man, Fred Long, and to Dallas Fisher for his lazy Susan.

To the people at North Light Books for their guidance, patience and cooperation. This book required many helping hands, not the least of which belong to Jennifer Long, our editor, and Christine Polomsky, our photographer. We want you to know how much we appreciate your hard work and patience! We learned a lot!

From Bobbie to Annette Dozier—thanks for being there through the birth of this book. You are my rock.

Table of Contents

Projects to Get You Started

Here are eleven decorative painting projects incorporating the lettering styles
you've just learned. Try out your new-found skills with these ideas, then add
your own professional-looking lettering to all of your projects.

82

GLOSSARY
Unfamiliar with a term? Find the definition here.

SAYINGS AND QUOTATIONS
300 charming quotes and one-liners you can add to your own projects.

RESOURCES

INDEX

Introduction

Hi! My name is Bobbie Gray and this is my husband, Jim. As far back as I can remember, I wanted to draw and paint. I couldn't draw enough, especially horses. My grandmother always encouraged me to pursue my artistic talents and helped me as I grew. "Draw enough horses," she said, "and some day you will become a teacher and have your summers off to paint all you wish." (Which makes me think, when do I start getting my summers off?)

I took as many art courses in school as I could—I even flunked geometry because I was always drawing in class.

After Jim and I got married, my art career was put on hold while we raised six children. I still painted a lot of furniture and walls, sometimes surprising Jim when he came home and found the walls painted halfway, or the commode seat painted a different color with flowers on it. "You painted what?" he would laugh and say, but never stopped me. My desire to paint increased more and more. (Now it has expanded to customizing designs on walls and furniture.)

After our sixth child was born, the older children became built-in baby-sitters for the smaller kids while I took classes in earnest.

Soon I was teaching classes at my dining room table to friends who wanted to learn the basics of decorative painting. (Didn't all of us older gals start that way? And wasn't it great fun?)

Since that time, I've had the opportunity to paint with some really great teachers, read some wonderful books and learn from many fine video tapes on decorative painting.

Just when you think you know it all, there is more to learn. And, basically, that's what we'd like to present to you—something new! An easy and simplified way to enhance your painted boxes, plaques, walls or furniture.

Over the years, we have decorated with lettering many of the projects that we create and teach. Written messages enhance most any decorative work because words add another dimension. All the paintings and statues in museums have titles for the viewer's benefit—for viewers to instantly gain an insight into the artist's perspective.

In teaching decorative painting classes, we have discovered the need for guidance in the area of lettering. Why should we paint a spectacular project and not be entirely assured that the lettering we use is of the same quality as the finished product?

Many of our painting students have asked, "Can I do that?" or "What will it take for me to learn to add lettering to my artwork?" As a result, we put our heads together and have put in print the *whys* and *wherefores* of interested students and casual observers.

Take a little journey through the pages of our book. Your final destination will be the ability to do brush-stroke lettering with ease—a whole new skill.

Jim and I are both professionals at what we do. I have been awarded the degree of Certified Decorative Artist (CDA) from the Society of Decorative Painters and have passed my Master Tray, part of the certification program for becoming a Master Decorative Artist.

I've spent over twenty-five years painting and teaching in the decorative field. I've taught at many national decorative painting conventions, as well as local and national seminars, and have a home studio in St. Charles, Missouri, where I teach several classes a week to students of all skill levels.

Over the years I have developed a pattern packet business and published two books with Jim on decorative painting and lettering.

Jim is a professional sign and sketch artist with over forty years of experience designing, selling and making signs for many national companies. Jim's father operated an outdoor advertising plant, where Jim spent summers in the sign apprentice program while he went to high school and college.

He has taught sign-painting at a national trade school and knows what it takes to design and letter professionally.

Jim is one of a dying breed. Newcomers are not attracted to the craft because computers have caught up with the sign-painting field, making quality signs at a good speed, albeit higher costs.

Jim will show you techniques and tricks of the trade not put in print before that will further your ability to make quality letters.

I have watched Jim paint signs over the years, and would often remark, "I wish I could do that." He always replied that anyone could do it if they spent some practice time using a simple variation of what he called speed lettering.

Out of these sessions we have developed a technique of numbered brushstrokes to teach artists of all levels how to enhance their finished products, whether it be on canvas, paper, wood or furniture.

Many happy students encouraged me to expand teaching the alphabets by putting together the lessons in book form. So here we are.

The techniques shown in this book will be those that are actually used commercially in the sign business. Therefore, *they all work!* You will find many uses for these techniques in the future.

Our aim is not to make sign painters of you, but rather to aid your recognition of what constitutes accurate and clean lettering. What we do will be basic, but can always be embellished with "doodads" or "gingerbread" for different effects.

As we have taught lettering to decorative artists, we have collected the answers to many valuable questions about the various aspects of lettering, i.e., strokes, size, scale, etc. We propose to pass this information on to you.

We hope that you enjoy the ideas presented in this book, and have many opportunities to use them.

Tools and Supplies

"Where do I go?" and "How do I get started?" are two of the most asked questions about learning anything, much less learning to paint letters. Good artisans and craftsmen the world over know the meaning of proper tools and their value in making a quality product. Some of the supplies can be substituted; others are optional but might make the job easier if they are available when you need them.

Thank goodness most tools and supplies for acrylic and enamel painting are readily available at most art stores. In some areas the local hardware stores have all the supplies you might need. Either of these mediums can be used to learn the basic lettering strokes. You are not limited to any one medium, so try both of the techniques and choose the method you like best.

Layout and Transferring Supplies

Bienfang 20 lb. White Poster Layout Paper
This will be used to make rough layouts. You can make all the mistakes you want on this paper, rather than experimenting on more costly surfaces.

Gray and White Transfer Paper
Use this paper to imprint the outline of the copy by placing it between the pattern and the prepared surface. Using a tracing tool or stylus, transfer the copy to the surface. Don't press so hard as to dent the project surface.

Tracing Paper
Also sometimes called vellum or parchment paper. See-through paper for tracing. Can be painted on for practice without wrinkling.

No. 2 Soft Lead Pencils, Soft Stick Charcoal and White Chalk
It will be much easier to draw and erase your layout with these soft leads.

Art Gum, Pink Pearl or Kneaded Rubber Eraser
These soft erasers will prevent tearing when erasing, which can ruin a good paper layout.

These items are available at art supply stores everywhere.

These are the proper supplies to make things easier.

Stylus

This is a metal, pencil-like tool with ball tips on either end that enables you to trace over the copy without distorting the layout on the pattern. The stylus will transfer the copy to the project surface with a light touch.

Offset Ruler

An offset ruler is constructed of two pieces of wood with a thin metal strip protruding along the entire length. It can be used to draw straight lines and to measure distances. The offset ruler is also an aid in painting straight lines with a brush. When you pull the brush against the metal edge paint cannot seep under it. This type of ruler is the only one that will achieve this result.

You may also find a T-square handy for making right angles.

Pounce Wheel

A pounce wheel is a metal wheel with star-point edges and a handle, used for perforating paper patterns and layouts. They are available at any art supply or fabric store that carries X-Acto tools.

Pounce Bag

A piece of old cotton cloth or sock filled with powdered charcoal or chalk. (Use charcoal for light surfaces and white chalk for dark surfaces.) Patting this bag over the perforations in your pattern will reproduce your layout as often as you wish, instead of you having to retrace every time.

A piece of jumbo soft charcoal will serve the same purpose if rubbed over the perforations. A fine dust will form over the holes and can be patted in with any piece of cloth or paper towel.

Old Newspapers

Preferably the want ads. Newsprint is a cheap and readily available practice surface. Turned sideways, the column lines make excellent guidelines for practicing your strokes.

These rulers are absolutely necessary to form proper letters.

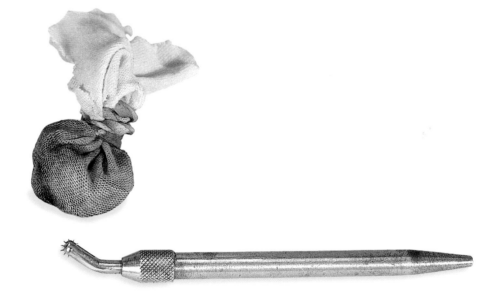

While optional, the pounce wheel will help you make quality reproductions.

Brushes

We primarily use Royal Langnickel brushes from Royal & Langnickel Brush Manufacturing of Merrillville, Indiana. We find a great consistency throughout the brush line, whether we are painting with oil paints or acrylics. Most quality art supply stores have the brushes in stock. In some areas you may need to find a sign-painting supply house. There are, of course, different brushes for different mediums.

Acrylic Brushes
- Langnickel series 2040, no. 4 and no. 6
- Royal Golden Taklon series RG 595
- Royal series RG 585 liners 5/0, no. 1 and no. 2

Oil Brushes
- Langnickel series 1300, no. 0 through no. 12 (The larger the letter, the higher the number.)

We prefer to use Langnickel Quills because the quill-style brush carries enough paint to make complete strokes evenly, regardless of the length of the stroke.

Acrylic Brushes
These are used with acrylic paints.

Caring for Your Brushes

Jim and I cannot stress enough the importance of good brush care. We both make sure our brushes are cleaned thoroughly and stored properly after each painting session. Some of Jim's brushes are twenty-five years old and still usable because of the good care and the quality of the brushes.

I rinse my brushes thoroughly in my brush basin with clean water. If I am not going to use them for awhile, I clean them with Deco Magic brush cleaner, reshape the bristles and leave the cleaner in the brush until I use the brush again.

Jim uses paint thinner to clean his brushes because he prefers to letter with enamel paint. He then dresses and reshapes his brushes with lard oil. This keeps the moths away and helps keep the brushes flexible.

Oil Brushes
These are the proper brushes to use with enamel paints.

Paints

DecoArt Americana Acrylic Paints

These paints work well on our projects. They flow off the brushes with the type of consistency needed to pull through the strokes of the letters. This major brand is available at any art supply store. Paint with any colors for practice.

1-Shot Lettering Enamels

These enamels are easy to use and ideal for any projects that require a durable finish because of extreme weather conditions. They are long lasting and have good opacity, giving the lettering a smooth, glossy finish. There is no need to varnish over this paint to make it last. All colors are available in 4 oz. (112g) cans and are usually found in sign supply stores, if not available at your favorite stores.

1-Shot Poster Colors

The poster colors, which dry to a flat (or non-shiny) finish, also make excellent working colors. Since both the enamels and the poster colors must be thinned with turpentine or mineral spirits, the working conditions and cleanup are not much different.

The colors needed will be dictated by the color schemes you have in mind for your projects.

Americana Paints
Bobbie prefers painting with acrylic paints.

1-Shot Enamels
Jim prefers painting with enamels.

Setting Up a Workspace

A good surface to work on is probably the foremost item to have. Our studio includes both a flat table and a drawing board made of Upsom Board—available at most old-time lumber yards—giving us a flat surface and also one that will support thumbtacks. Plywood also works well, since it is readily available. We like to pin our layout and any relevant notes to the drawing board.

Our wall-mounted board angles upward to the rear by about fifteen degrees in order to make it easier for us to reach items and draw our layouts. An old yardstick tacked to the lower edge of the board keeps pencils and other tools from rolling off and also gives us a measuring tool.

If you are already set up with a solid surface that you do not care to mar or damage, simply place several sheets of cardboard on top of each other. This way a thumbtack can be placed with ease (the use of thumbtacks will be explained in the Tricks of the Trade section).

General Supplies

Paper Towels
The more absorbent towels serve a purpose when cleaning brushes, since they are soft and will not damage the hair in the brushes. The towels are nice to have handy if a spill occurs or just for cleaning your hands.

Scotch Magic Tape
Paint will not seep under the edges of this tape, offering cleaner edges when needed for both letters and borders.

Illustration or Bristol Board
Low-cost cardstock is available almost anywhere from supermarkets to art supply stores. This makes an excellent surface for practicing layouts and lettering strokes. All paints seem to flow well on this type of surface without wrinkling the material.

Thumbtacks
To hold paper and perform layout shortcuts.

Fine Sandpaper
To sand the backs of perforated patterns.

Masking Tape
Any size, for general uses such as holding patterns.

Water Basin
For acrylic brush cleaning.

36-inch (1m) Straightedge
For measuring long distances.

Cans
Used (and washed) tuna or cat food cans to mix paints and clean brushes.

Thread
Heavy-duty thread, kite string or picture wire will be used in the Tricks of the Trade section.

General Supplies

Basic Brushstrokes

Anyone who has ever picked up a paintbrush of any kind, even a house painter, knows the importance of making good strokes. In the lettering field it is imperative that we learn to feel the strokes that form the parts of the letters. The only way to develop the feel of the strokes is to practice, practice, practice.

We have developed a practice technique that will transform the normal drudgery of practice into fun. As you paint these strokes over and over you should develop the firmness and feel of the letter strokes. You will see the progress occur as you notice how the brush becomes a tool in your hand. Familiarity with the brush in your hand will make practice easy. Forming some letters that look good to you will encourage you to practice further.

So let's get to it and enjoy learning brushstrokes.

Making Your First Strokes

I'm sure you have wondered why we listed old newspapers in our supply lists. It's a great way to practice your strokes without using up a lot of good cardstock or paper. Surely you would rather mess up old want ads than paper or wood pieces? The newspaper also protects the table or easel you are working on. This is a new way to recycle!

Turn the want ads sideways—see how the columns make great guidelines for practicing horizontal brushstrokes? The vertical lines are then formed by the want ad print. The want ads have lots of small columns you can practice on, making them more useful than the other pages.

You can be as messy as you want with your beginning strokes and still not have to clean up. The paper surface may be more absorbent than you usually paint on, but it will help you get the feel of the strokes and the way the brush performs. You should take to this quite readily. We will show you how easy it is to be bold with your strokes and make letters with a series of vertical, horizontal and modified round moves.

Thinning the Paint

To thin acrylic paint, put a quarter-sized puddle of paint on the palette pad. Mix water with the paint to achieve the consistency needed for the paint to flow off the brush.

Push the tip of the brush down on the palette pad, spreading the end of the brush to hold more paint.

If the paint is too thick, the stroke will be difficult to finish. If it is too

Use the old newspaper want ads to practice your strokes.

Thin acrylic paint to the proper consistency on the palette.

thin, the paint will run. Experience will help you find the right consistency.

Whether he is using acrylic, enamels or poster paints, Jim likes to mix enough paint for the entire project to the consistency he wants in an old tuna can. This is a good technique, because the paint is always the right consistency. He dips the brush, then pushes the heel of the brush on the edge of the can to spread the hairs.

Holding the Brush

Hold the brush gently between your index finger and first finger, with the handle of the brush resting on the middle finger. Rest the little finger on the surface as a guide for a full, firm stroke. Hold the brush almost perpendicular to the surface. For most of these exercises a no. 5 or no. 6 brush is used.

Push down firmly with the tip of the brush in order to spread the hair for a full-width stroke. Using your entire hand, pull down to make the stroke. This gives you the firmness and the boldness to make the full stroke without making a wavy line. Jim always says, "Lean on the brush."

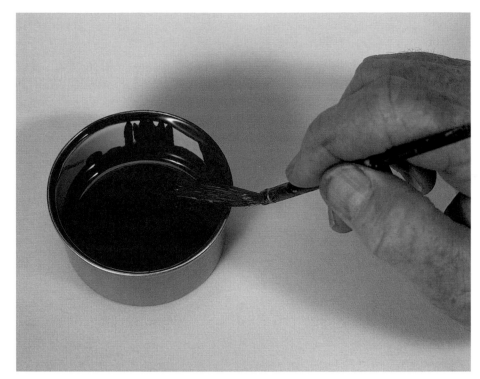
Jim mixes his paint to the proper consistency in a can.

This is the proper way to hold your brush whether you're painting in enamels or acrylics.

Practicing Vertical Strokes

First, practice vertical strokes to get the feel of the brush. Make firm, bold strokes, leaving some space between the strokes and repeating the stroke over and over.

Continue to practice until you can start the stroke evenly on the top line and finish the stroke evenly on the bottom line.

Don't be careful—be bold and smooth. Try to make the width of each stroke the same, with the same area between strokes. Perform at least ten to twenty strokes. You will see more improvement the more you practice the strokes.

As you pull through the strokes you should notice that it is not the tip of the brush that finishes the stroke. It is the paint from the middle to the tip of the brush. If the top and bottom of the stroke are not slightly rounded, go ahead and use the tip of the brush to give them a casual look. It is all right to have brush marks at the end of your stroke.

Practicing Horizontal Strokes

Next, perform the same number of horizontal strokes, staying within the lines. You can place a center stroke (as though you were making an **E**).

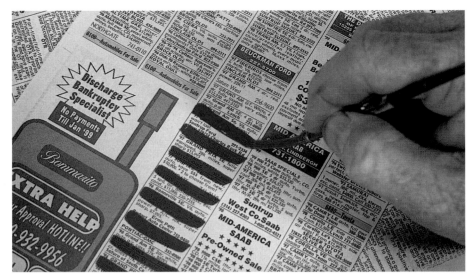

Vertical Strokes
Using the want ads, practice the strokes using the columns laid horizontally. (I turn mine at a slight angle.) Use the top line and the bottom line as guides.

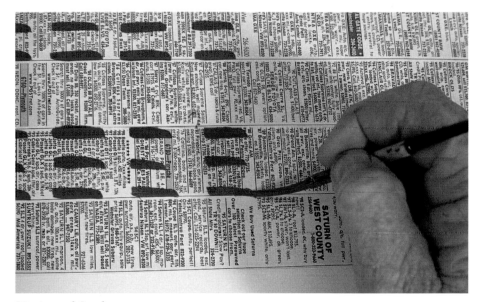

Horizontal Strokes
Hold the brush sideways and use the column lines for guides. Be sure to press firmly and pull the brush through until you feel the stroke.

Practicing Curved Strokes

Basically, there are only two major curved strokes in this technique that require practice. These strokes should cover most of the round letters.

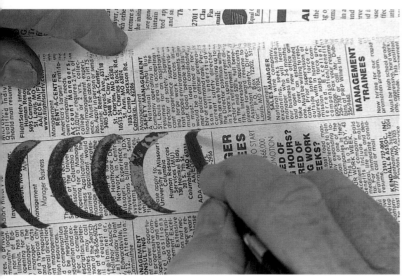

1. *The Left Curve*
Start with the tip of the brush and pull down and to the left.

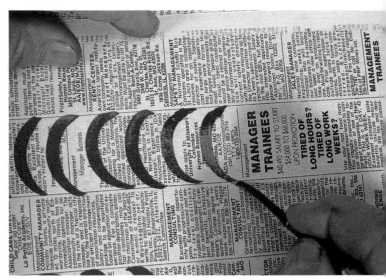

2. End with the tip of the brush

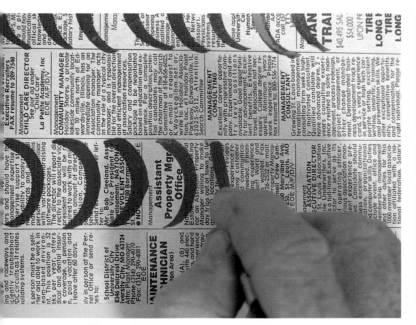

1. *The Right Curve*
Place the tip of the brush on the top line and pull to the right.

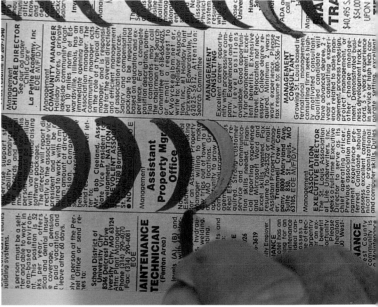

2. End with the tip of the brush

Using the Strokes to Form Your First Letter

After practicing the curved strokes several times, try forming the letter **O**. This is a casual brushstroke, so it will have a smooth flow to it. Round letters can and should go a little above and below the top and bottom guidelines. The letter **O** does not have to be perfectly round, but the sides should be as symmetrical as possible.

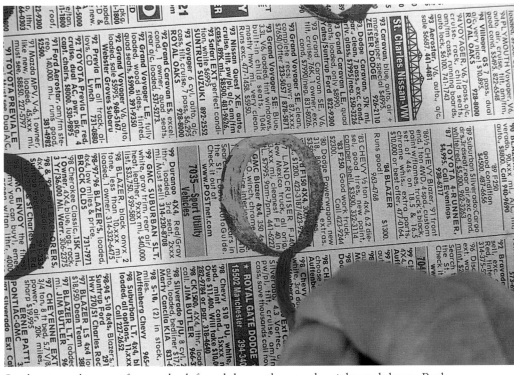

Stroke top to bottom, first to the left and down, then to the right and down. Both strokes end with the tip of the brush.

Make as many letters as you want, concentrating on the strokes. Try to keep the **O**s round; avoid making letters shaped like horse collars. You may want to try various widths of the letter, too.

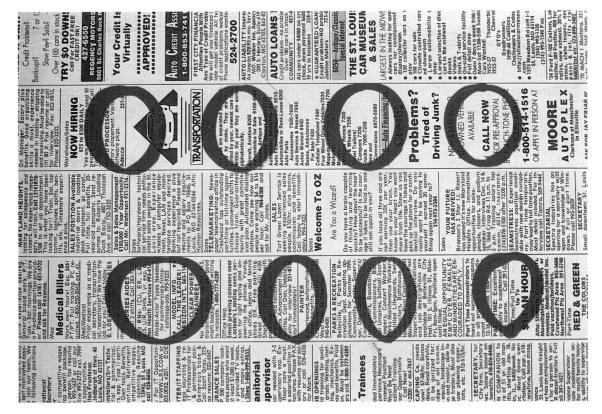

Painting a Letter **S**

The letter **S** is made with a stroke of its own. As you practice, you will notice how it looks and how easy it is to make

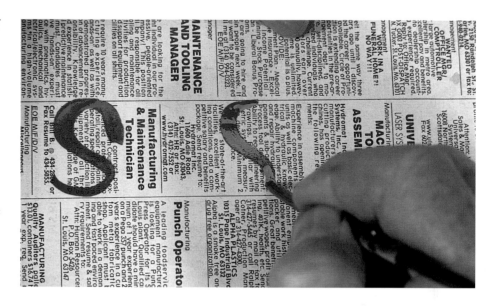

1. Start with the tip of the brush. Place it on the top line, then pull left, then down until about halfway down, then slant to the right until about three-fourths of the way down.

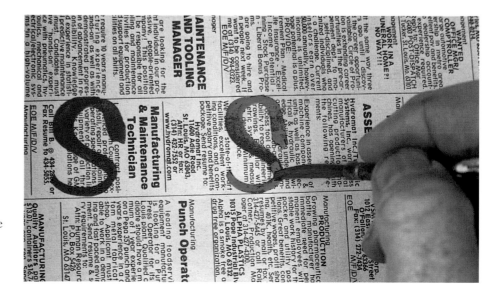

2. The second stroke is simply performed by placing the brush where you started the first stroke and pulling down to the right, pressing fully until the brush is about one-third of the way down. Then lift the brush.

3. The third stroke simply starts on the left and curves to join the first stroke. Use less pressure so the stroke is thinner.

Using Connectors to Form Letters

While you are concentrating on the width of your practice strokes, try also to leave the same space between the strokes so you can go back and actually form letters while practicing. That's when you will see how easy making letters is!

As you see in the pictures on pages 23–25, the connecting lines forming letters, especially in the lowercase letters, do not require any flipping of the brush or wrist. The letter can be formed by using the tip of the brush.

This is another practice exercise that should be performed over and over. Many of these connecting lines can be made with the brush held in the same manner. Don't try to twist the brush; hold it in a sideways manner or use only the tip of the brush.

It is important that you pay attention to where the connecting strokes join letters. The average novice fails to connect letters high enough.

Here's your chance to form your first uppercase word. It uses basically straight strokes.

As you become more proficient with your vertical strokes, have a little fun and try forming the word **PUMPKIN** by only adding a few connecting strokes. We call these "connectors" because they *connect* the main strokes together to form a letter.

You should at this point form the words **minimum** and **pumpkin** (see next page) in lowercase letters in order to practice small connecting lines. You are forming words already. Are you paying attention to the connector strokes? Note how high up they join the downstrokes.

Your goal is to make your strokes look as much alike as possible. Letters can be a little off in character, but make each **A** look like all other **A**s and each **E** look like all other **E**s.

Crossbars should also be consistent in placement. Strive for consistency in the formation of all your letters. Remember this takes practice! While this is a casual and forgiving way to paint letters, consistency is the key.

I'm sure you will have fun practicing the casual strokes as you begin to feel the various moves. Make some vertical strokes allowing a slight curve to the right from top to bottom. Allow yourself the freedom to let the stroke flow. Remember this is a casual alphabet.

Make some connecting strokes once in a while and enjoy the pleasure of forming a letter.

Make all the mistakes you want on the want ads. You will find a little paint goes a long way toward learning this alphabet.

Remember, practice makes perfect, so try the words several times and notice how each time the word has a cleaner and sharper appearance. Now isn't that fun?

From this point of the exercise, we can go forward and make some letters using the alphabets in section three. For your convenience, each letter will be presented in numbered strokes. We hope you like this learning technique.

Don't take a shortcut with the connectors. Study the different look between the letters on the right and the ones on the left. Correctly performed, the strokes give a pleasant character to the letters and make them look professionally done.

Easy Alphabets

Now let's try making some letters so we can see the similarities between the strokes that are used in different letters. As you progress you will see how **A**, **V**, **W**, **M**, **X**, **Y** and **Z** have similar, modified straight strokes. The more you practice the letters, the easier the alphabet will be. As you have probably noticed, this style of lettering is merely a series of straight and slightly rounded strokes connected to form letters.

The Basic Alphabet

This is the standard alphabet from which you will work and practice. Each stroke is color-coded to show the order in which it was made (see legend below right). We don't expect you to use these colors to paint your alphabet; this is just to help you determine the flow of forming letters.

Work with one letter at a time. Stroke the same letter several times.

When you have doubts, always refer to this alphabet. Many of the same strokes are used in both the upper- and lowercase alphabets.

For your convenience, we have lettered an alphabet step by step in both upper- and lowercases starting on page 30. You can see from the photos how each stroke of the brush is made.

Refer to page 61 for more information on terms like cap line, waistline and base line, which will be used in the following pages.

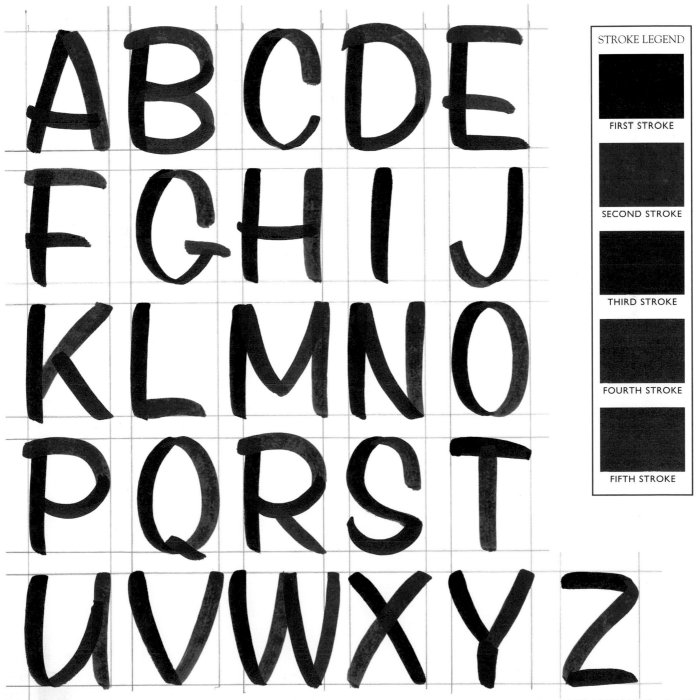

STROKE LEGEND

FIRST STROKE

SECOND STROKE

THIRD STROKE

FOURTH STROKE

FIFTH STROKE

abcde
fghij
klmno
pqrst
uvwxy

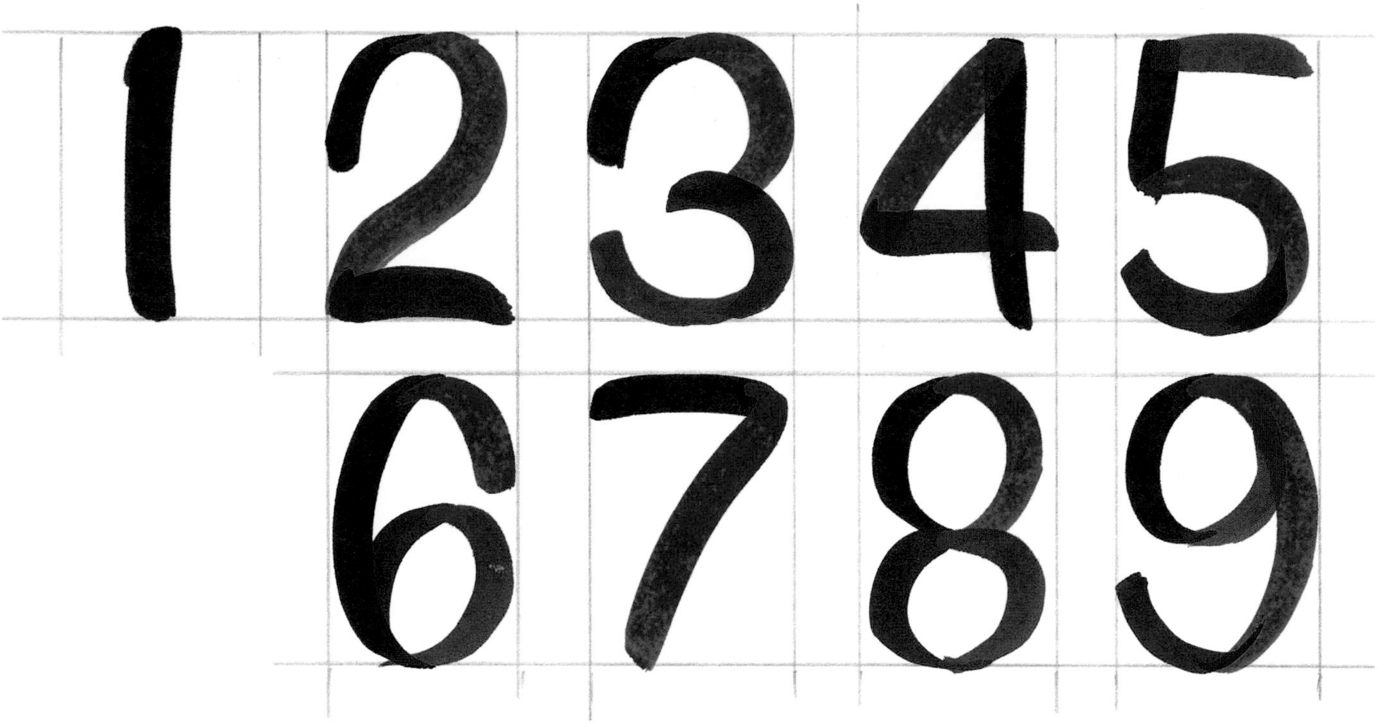

1 2 3 4 5
6 7 8 9

The Benefit of Casual Lettering

Letters in an artwork serve as more than identification. They convey to the beholder an idea in advance of viewing the entire artwork.

While we want the viewers to get an idea of the project, we don't want the letters to take attention away from the art. We don't want the letters to be seen above the artwork, but to blend into the entire piece—to become part of it. So we keep the letters simple without too many flourishes or "doodads."

Merely slanting the letters of an alphabet or using all uppercase or all lowercase letters can enhance a message and convey emphasis. We can also widen letters or increase their height for effect or for spacing.

Once you're familiar with the basic alphabet, you can easily paint any variation of the casual brushstroke letters.

*The Basic Uppercase Alphabet
Step by Step*

Use one column of the want ads to paint these letters. The top line of the column will be the cap line and the bottom line of the column will be the base line.

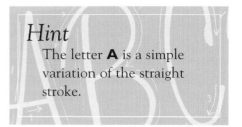

1. Push down on the brush and pull the slightly slanted stroke from 12 o'clock to 7 o'clock.

2. Repeat the stroke from 12 o'clock to 5 o'clock.

3. Pull the crossbar from left to right, keeping the stroke below the center of the letter.

1. Pull the stroke vertically as you have practiced.

2. Turn the brush in your fingers about three-fourths of the way around and pull the brush to the right about halfway down the letter. Don't try to make the full stroke back to the vertical bar. Using only the tip of the brush, complete the loop by pulling the brush to join step 1. At this point you have completed the letter **P**, connecting to the vertical bar slightly below center. If you were to pull a stroke from this stroke to the base line you would form the letter **R**.

3. Make the same two strokes as in step 2. The lower loop will be smaller, yet wider, than the top loop. You have now completed the full letter **B**.

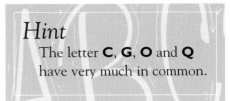

Hint
The letter **C**, **G**, **O** and **Q** have very much in common.

1. Place the brush on the cap line, pushing down slightly. As you pull the brush to the left and downward, add pressure to widen the brush. Continue pulling the brush to the base line as indicated.

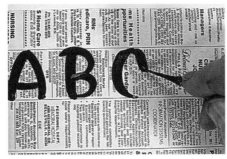

2. Place the brush on the cap line again, press, and pull the brush firmly to the right until almost halfway down the letter. This same stroke will be used in the letters **G** and **Q**.

3. Finish the letter with the tip of the brush, pulling downward to the base line.

1. Make the same downstroke as for the **B**: cap to base line.

2. This is the same stroke you practiced when making your first letter **O** on page 21.

3. Use the tip of your brush turned sideways, but use less pressure.

1. Pull through with the vertical stroke.

2. Pull from left to right with the brush turned about three-fourths in your fingers to form both the top bar and the bottom bar. Slightly turn the brush in your fingers to finish the strokes.

3. You can now gauge where to put the center bar; it should be slightly lower than center.

1. Start with the downstroke we've practiced.

2. Hold the brush sideways as you did for the **E**.

3. Form this stroke on the same level as for the **E**.

1. Use the **C** downstroke, then pull.

2. Make the full **C** as you did before.

3. Turn this **C** into a **G** with a low cross-stroke.

1. Push the brush down and pull down.

2. Make a second stroke identical to the first.

3. Use the tip of your brush to make a thin, low crossbar.

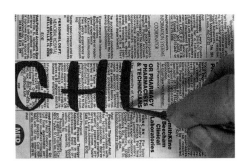

1. This letter is simply a downstroke.

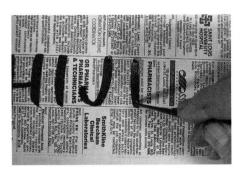

1. Start with an **I** downstroke.

2. Add the head of the **J** with the tip of the brush turned sideways.

1. Start with the downstroke.

2. Pull this stroke about two-thirds of the way down the first, as if you're forming the leg of an **A**.

3. Pull this leg down to form a **K**.

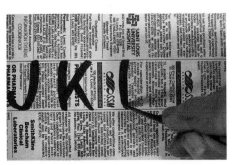

1. Start with the basic downstroke.

2. Add a stroke at the base.

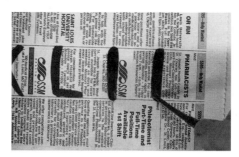

1. Make the two vertical strokes wider than in other letters to leave space for downstrokes.

2.

3. Pull down left to right, laying the brush on the downstroke to start. You may or may not go to the base line.

4. This stroke finishes the **M**; keep about the same amount of space on either side of the center.

1. The letter **N** is simply three downstrokes.

2.

3.

1. This is why you practiced curved strokes. Make the left stroke first. Start with the tip of the brush, then push to widen the brush. Let up on the pressure as you end the curves on the base line.

2.

1. The **P** is made just like the first two steps of the **B**.

2.

1. The letter **Q** is an **O** with a free-flowing tail.

2.

3.

1. Pull a basic downstroke.

2. Start on the tip of the brush, pulling to the right. Flatten the brush as the stroke widens, then return to the tip as you end the stroke.

3. Pull this stroke at about 40° to the right. Make it a bold stroke.

1. Place the tip of the brush on the cap line and pull it left as shown. As you start making the curve, push down on the brush and let the stroke happen. Lighten the pressure as you change the stroke direction to the right and stop about three-fourths of the way down. Make this move without twisting the brush.

2. The upper stroke is made by putting the tip of the brush on the cap line and moving it to the right and down until about halfway. Don't be afraid to push on the brush. When you reach the halfway point the stroke should be formed with a little twist or movement to the right at the end.

3. This way the tip of the brush finishes the stroke about three-fourths of the way down. The bottom stroke, then, is almost like a connector stroke. There is almost a rhythm in making this down-stroke of an **S**, and you'll feel it the more you try it.

1. The letter **T** is always started with a crossbar. Turn the brush sideways, pulling from left to right. Push down, spreading the bristles and twist slightly downward to complete the stroke.

2. Now place the brush in the center of the crossbar and pull down firmly to complete.

Hint
Let's spend some more time forming the top curves of the **C** and the **S**. There's a subtle move to the right and down that is used in both letters.

1. Press the brush down and make a full stroke. The roundness of the stroke at the end is formed by letting up on the pressure.

2. Duplicate the previous stroke, allowing room to approximate the letter width.

3. Using the tip of the brush, pull from about halfway down the second stroke and round off at the first stroke.

1. Press the tip on the cap line and pull the stroke with a curve to about 5 o'clock.

2. Repeat with the tip on the cap line and pull to about 7 o'clock. Release the pressure at the end of the stroke.

1. The letter **W** is naturally a wider letter and almost like making two **V**s.

2. Complete the first **V**.

3. Start the second **V** with the same roundness at the end.

4. Finish the second **V** as shown to form the letter.

1. Place the tip on the cap line at about 11 o'clock and pull to the base line, slightly rounding the letter to the left.

2. Pull this stroke much like the first stroke on the letter **A**. Keep the roundness as you pull to the right at the end.

1. Pull this stroke toward 4 o'clock, stopping two-thirds of the way down and rounding slightly.

2. Pull to the left toward 8 o'clock, joining the first stroke.

3. Make a basic downstroke.

1. This letter is like making two cross-bar strokes like the **T** or **E**. Make the top first.

2. Use the base line as a guide. Make the same length as the top stroke.

3. Place the brush on the right of the top stroke and pull through to the left of the bottom stroke.

The Basic Lowercase Alphabet Step by Step

At this point you can use the strokes you have practiced to make lowercase or small letters. Some additional strokes will be required, but since the letters are so much like basic handwriting, you should find these exercises more fun.

These strokes should be practiced on the newspaper again using only one column for the height. This time think of the top line of the column as your waistline (see page 61). Letters like **b**, **g**, **k**, **l** and **y** will require two lines and will extend above or below the lines. Use the paper up—it's cheap.

It should be evident from the following pictures that many strokes are duplicated in different letters, as in **a**, **b**, **d**, **g**, **p** and **q**. Notice how the alphabet indicates the position of the connectors. Give them the room to be consistent

1. Place the tip of the brush at the waistline and pull to the left, making an arc. Finish firmly without twisting the brush, releasing pressure at the base line.

2. Use the tip of the brush to make a small pull to the right to about one-fourth of the way down the column. This will aid you in gauging the size of the letter.

3. Place the tip of the brush a little below the waistline at the edge of the second stroke and push down firmly, pulling down to the base line.

4. Using the tip of the brush, pull down and left from one-third of the way up the downstroke. Use less pressure, joining the first stroke at the base line.

5. With the tip of the brush, add the finishing touch by pulling from the right down to the left. Start about one-third of the way above the base line. This adds class to the letter.

1. Place the tip about halfway up the column above and pull firmly down to the base line. Use pressure, releasing at the bottom.

2. Put the brush on the waistline and pull to the first stroke.

3. Add the stroke from the right down to the left, joining at the bottom.

1. From top to bottom, pull the stroke to the left.

2. Add the top of the **c** by using the tip of the brush and pulling to the right almost one-third of the way down the column. Let up without using the tip.

3. Finish the letter with the tip of the brush from right to left, rounding off the bottom.

1. This letter is the **a** with a longer downstroke.

2. You will see similar strokes to these in the **p** and **g**.

3.

4. The tip of the brush is used to form this stroke, pulling from the right to the left. Start at least one-third of the way up the column.

5. Use the tip of the brush to finish off this letter, right to left, rounding the bottom.

1. The curved stroke can start above the waistline and finish below the base line for good shape.

2. Using the tip of the brush, connect to the first stroke and pull right to about halfway down the column.

3. Complete the oval with the tip of the brush from left to right. Don't try to make the oval with one stroke.

4. Finish the letter with the tip of the brush, pulling right to left.

1. From above the waistline, pull the stroke down, pressing firmly to spread the bristles. Let up the pressure as you get below the base line and pull slightly right for roundness.

2. This stroke starts one-third of the way above the base line. Using the tip of the brush, pull down and to the right, curving left to round out the letter.

3. Complete the letter with the tip of the brush, right to left.

1. Curve the stroke from the top to the bottom, as in the letter **a**.

2. This stroke sets the width of the letter.

3. This basic downstroke reaches below the base line and curves to the left at the end.

4. From one-third up the column, use the tip of the brush to join the strokes. Keep the roundness.

5. Finish off with the tip of the brush, left to right.

1. Press firmly and start at least one-third above the waistline, pulling full to the base line.

2. Use the waist- and base lines as guides.

3. Press firmly and pull right to left to at least halfway down the column width.

4. Add the tail with a curved stroke from right to left.

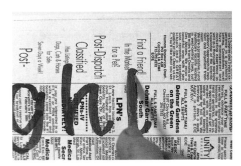

1. Pull down to the base line.

2. Finish the letter with the tip of the brush, pulling from right to left.

3. Dot the **i** with a dab of paint. Don't be careful, be casual.

1. Press the brush to the waistline and pull down below the base line, curving left and releasing pressure at the end.

2. Add this stroke with the tip of the brush, pulling left to right. Round the bottom of the strokes.

3. Use a casual dab of paint to dot the **j**.

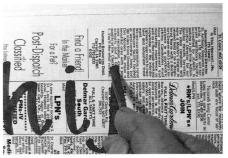

1. Pull down from above the waistline.

2. Slant from the upper right down to the left, about one-third of the way above the base line.

3. Pull down at 5 o'clock to the base line.

4. Finish the letter with the tip of the brush.

1. Start with a casual, straight stroke.

2. Add the finishing stroke with the tip of the brush, moving right to left.

1. Start with a basic stroke but make it wider than the others, like you did for the capital **M**.

2. Allow room for the second stroke.

3. This stroke should make the letter about 50% wider than a normal letter.

4. Place the tip on the second stroke and pull down right to left with a slight arc to at least halfway down the column.

5. Repeat the process between the third and second strokes.

6. Add the small flourish to finish off the letter.

1. This letter is almost a repeat of the **m**. Continue to be casual with your brush.

2.

3.

4.

1. Place the tip of your brush slightly above the waistline, pull left and apply pressure, spreading the bristles as you widen the arc. Release pressure as you reach the base line.

2. Put the tip on top of the first stroke. Pull right, increasing pressure, and finish to the left, joining the thin strokes at the base line.

3. Finish off the letter with the tip of the brush, pulling from right to left.

1. Pull down below the base line about halfway in to the next column.

2. Place the tip of the brush slightly above the waistline and pull to the left.

3. Place the tip of the brush on the waistline and pull right, pressing for width to the base line.

4. Put the tip of the brush on the first stroke about one-fourth of the way up from the base line and pull to the right, finishing about one-fourth of the way up the column.

1. This is another letter with the basic **a** shape. Pull the top to the bottom, curved stroke.

2. Add the top stroke from left to right, as was done on the letter **c**. This stroke is repeated many times in the alphabet.

3. Pull down to below the base line with a curve to the left as pressure decreases.

4. Using the tip of the brush, pull down to the left and curve to join the down-stroke.

5. Add with the tip, then stroke from above the line to join the third stroke.

6. Put the finishing touch on with the tip of the brush, from left to right.

1. Use the tip of the brush to pull a thin line from above the waistline down to about 7 o'clock.

2. Put the tip on the first stroke, push down and pull to the right, then pull down and right all in one stroke.

3. Finish with the tip from right to left.

1. The tip of the brush makes this stroke, curving right to left.

2. Place the tip at the top of the first stroke, press and pull down to the base line with a slight left curve.

3. With the tip of the brush, make this curving cross-stroke. Finish about one-fourth of the way up from the base line.

1. Make the stroke from slightly above the waistline, releasing pressure and curving to the right at the base line.

2. Add a flourish with the tip of the brush, pulling from right to left using the brush for roundness.

3. The crossbar can now be formed with the tip of the brush, or with a sideways full stroke. This is a good stroke with which to be casual.

1. This letter is like the uppercase **U**, only smaller. Casually form the first line curving slightly right.

2. Make the second stroke the same way.

3. Connect the stroke with the tip of your brush from halfway up the column, then to the base line.

4. Complete the letter with the tip of your brush.

1. Place the spread bristles on the waistline and pull down and right to the base line.

2. Use the tip to make a thin line from the top to the bottom, curving to the left. By now you should feel the paint itself making the curved bottoms of the letters.

3. Add a twist with the tip of the brush.

1. This letter is a **v** made half again as wide since **w** and **m** are wider than other letters. Curve the top to the bottom, left to right.

2. Use the tip for the stroke; the width is important.

3. Same as first stroke.

4. Use the tip to make this stroke.

5. Complete the letter with the tip of the brush for a real flourish.

1. Feel free to use a modified **S**-stroke (as in decorative painting), pulling from top left to right as the brush spreads.

2. The tip makes this stroke.

3. Finish with the tip.

1. Here's another example of straight strokes connecting—make the basic first stroke.

2. Press and pull down as you did with the **g**.

3. Connect with the brush tip, right to left. Start at least one-third of the way up the column.

4. Finish off with the tip of the brush, pulling from left to right.

1. Make a crossbar stroke.

2. Let the side of the brush make this letter.

3. A curved stroke is used in all round letters.

4. Finish the letter with the tip of the brush, pulling from left to right.

Variations on the Basic Alphabet

On the following pages are a couple of other alphabets that you can learn after spending some time practicing the series of strokes in the basic alphabet.

You will find that once you have learned the initial strokes, you can letter almost any alphabet. It is very important, though, that you study the letter constructions.

It will certainly help you to put vellum or parchment paper over the letters and duplicate them with your brush in hand. By now, after your practice, you should have some feel for the letter construction and the way the brush helps you make the strokes.

With each of the alphabets, we have also drawn numbered lines to help you learn the sequence of strokes.

It's a good idea to draw some lines from the top to the bottom of the want ads at about 15° and practice the same drills with strokes that form slanted letters. The technique of the strokes is the same, but there is a different feel. It's not difficult; try it and enjoy the learning experience.

After you have practiced the strokes and studied the letter formations, lay a sheet of parchment paper over the alphabet and paint the letters as though you were tracing. The parchment paper enables you to see the letter clearly in order to copy and the paper will not wrinkle. I love to see the happiness on my students' faces when they make the strokes over the parchment paper. If you have access to vellum paper, you can achieve the same results.

Bold Italic Alphabet
Here is the standard alphabet with an italic slant. It's fun to work with, and it's not as difficult as it may appear initially. The strokes are almost the same. Be sure to draw the slanted lines to guide your strokes. It is imperative that the strokes keep the same slant.

The main concern here is to keep the slant consistent from start to finish. On your layout, you should draw guidelines for consistency. This example was lettered with a no. 5 brush. Notice that almost all the strokes are the same width.

GHIJKLM

TUVWXYZ

Upright Script Lowercase Alphabet

Script letters, as shown, should be easier to learn in upright lettering. You will be using the basic strokes with hardly any variation.

abcdefghijklmn

opqrstuvwxyz

Thick-and-Thin Script Uppercase Alphabet

As you improve, we know you will want to do "thick-and-thin" lettering. This script always looks classy. Turn the paper slightly if you have any trouble. Feel how the brush works when going from the tip to the full spread of the hairs in forming letters. This is what is meant by leaning on the brush.

Upright Thin-Script Uppercase Alphabet

At first glance this alphabet may look difficult, but after you get into the strokework, you will find that the strokes are the basic ones learned at the beginning. The difference is that the tip of the brush is used exclusively. A liner brush is perfect for this style of letter.

g h i j k l m

t u v w x y z

Laying Out Your Lettering

The layout for your lettering is like a road map. You can wing it and hope you won't get lost, or you can plan your trip so that you will arrive at your destination when and where you like. There is no such thing as handlettering without some plan. Oh sure, there are experienced sign painters who have spent countless years perfecting their craft and have the ability to visualize their design. But even the experienced artist knows the value of a well-thought-out plan.

Planning Ahead

Every lettering project needs a plan, from the rough drawing to the finished product. It is not wise to venture forth without visualizing the area and overall space the letters will cover. Don't fall into the trap of not having enough space to finish your copy.

Start by determining the space you are trying to cover and finding the center. *Always* find the center. I once was painting a sign 15 feet (4.6m) high and 55 feet (16.8m) long, using a sketch prepared by another sketch man. Since I had used many of his sketches in the past, it never occurred to me to check the measurements. When I'd finished painting the letters, I realized the layout was only 50 feet (15.3m) in length. There I was with a full 5 feet (1.5m) of blank space left over. I felt upset and rather stupid when I saw all that white area. I failed to start in the center of the sign, so the job had to be completely painted out and lettered again. If I had started in the center, at least the white air space on each end of the lines of lettering would have been even and looked like it was planned.

Finding the Center

Determine the height and length of the lettering area. Find the center and try to visualize the message that will go in the area. Making a layout on a piece of paper will make the job much simpler. This will eventually become your pattern, which may be used over and over again. We generally use white poster bond paper.

cap line
waistline
center line
base line
descender line

center line

The center of this word theoretically would be between the **g** and **w**, but as you can see, it's not. Always check your layout.

Finding the center of the layout area should be a simple matter. Print out the copy that you intend to use. Suppose the word is **WIGWAM**. Draw the top and bottom lines for your guides. Then find the center of the word. Just counting the letters will not help you find the center, since all letters are not of the same width. **W**s, **M**s, and sometimes **O**s are wider than other letters. The letter **I** is much smaller than the standard-width letter.

An easy way to find the center when you lay out your copy is to fold the paper layout in half, with the outside left of the paper overlaying the outside right of the paper.

1. Measure the width of the area you want the lettering to fill. I placed the piece of board I want to letter on a piece of scrap paper and traced around it to make an accurately sized sketch.

2. Find the center of the area you want to letter.

4. Measure the top or cap line of the proposed line of letters.

3. Allow a border area to frame the copy area.

5. Allow the same amount of space between the bottom of the lower line of letters, or base line, and the border.

6. Draw the base line of the proposed letters. Leave space for the cap line of the next line of words if you will have more than one line.

Hint

Finding the center of the lettering involves more than just counting letters. Measuring the distance of the handwriting across the copy area is the only correct way, since all letters are not the same width, i.e., **W**, **I** or **M**.

Sketching Your Letters

After determining the centers of the layout, start sketching your letters. You will have air space above and below the letters, as well as on each end. This air space forms a sort of border to frame the lettering.

Draw just your cap or top line and your base line if you are going to use all capital letters. Use a T-square or ruler for straightness, or you can consult the Tricks of the Trade section for a shortcut method of drawing lines. As long as you are drawing lines and sketching on white paper, you can make your guidelines as heavy as you want.

Sketching the letters requires a lighter hand; each time you make a correction you can make the letter lines heavier. Keep in mind that you can always start over with a new sheet of paper.

Drawing the Waistline

A center line drawn horizontally will help determine where the cross-bar strokes will go with letters such as **E**, **F**, **P**, **R**, etc. This line will also aid you in structuring all the letters.

A waistline should be drawn if upper- and lowercase letters are to be used. A waistline is exactly what it might seem. It determines the height of the lowercase letter and should be slightly higher than center. Consult the examples for the proper format you will use.

In the beginning you must familiarize yourself with the letters of the alphabet. Pay attention to their size and structure. You may have preconceived ideas of what a letter looks like, and may be surprised how a letter is really constructed.

Hint
At this time we want to make it clear that all the lines drawn are guidelines and are not absolute lines. You are learning casual brushstroke lettering, so you have the freedom to wander slightly above and below the lines. You have the freedom to relax and not feel tension in forming your letters.

7. Lightly make a draft layout by using your natural handwriting or printing ability.

Hint

Several rough sketches may be necessary before you like the layout. If you are trying for a script-lettered work, handwrite your sketch for shape and spacing. Handwriting will be your best guide for letter size and overall shape. When you finish the sketch, be more specific with the shapes of the letters. Trust your capacity to visualize by printing or writing the complete word or message in the space allowed.

8. Measure the waistline approximately two-thirds of the way up for lowercase letters.

9. Carefully mark and draw the waistline for the lowercase letters.

10. Go over the handwriting, improving the layout with a darker impression. You can go over the letters as often as you wish. You can even use different colors or erase old lines.

11. You will finally settle on a finished look to the letters. Practice first—you'll get it.

Transferring the Sketch

When your layout is completed to your satisfaction, the white paper then becomes a pattern for repeated layouts. If you have multiple projects with the same copy, a pattern makes it easier to repeat that copy exactly. You have a choice of using transfer paper and a pencil or stylus to transfer the layout to your surface, or you can make a paper pounce pattern.

Pounce Method

We normally make a pounce pattern for all our projects. It makes the task easier. Try this technique and we are sure you will have fun reproducing layouts. If you are practicing on cheap paper, you can make as many mistakes as you want. The availability of the pounce pattern allows you to reproduce copy without making a new layout. Think of the time you will save not having to make another pencil layout each time.

You now may use your pattern many times over. You can pencil over the dust marks if you want, or you can make your strokes over the dotted lines. Brush the remaining dots off after the letters are complete and dry.

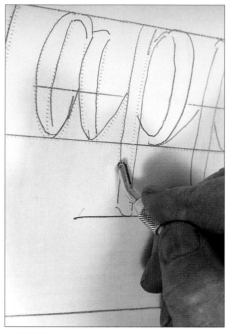

1. Make perforations by pressing the pounce wheel (a pencil-like tool with a pointed wheel on one end) over the lines you have drawn.

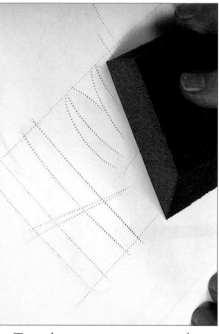

2. Turn the copy paper over and lightly sand the back with fine sandpaper.

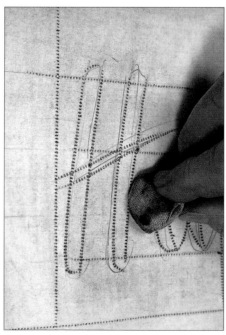

3. Using a charcoal or chalk-filled pounce bag, pat the powder through the holes that have been formed by the pounce wheel.

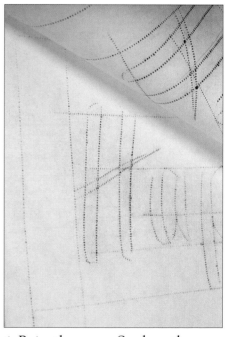

4. Raise the paper. See how the powder left the outline of your copy on the surface?

Drop Shadow

Once you have made your letters by pouncing with a paper pattern, paint them in. You can now add a three-dimensional look by creating drop shadows. Place your pounce pattern back over your painted lettering and then shift the paper down and to the left at least the width of your vertical stroke. Pounce the pattern again to form another outline of your letters. Now you can fill this area with a color that will contrast with the already painted letter. We call this shadowed letter a drop shadow. Always drop the shadow down and left. Keep in mind the light source is coming from the upper right.

If you started with a dark or bold colored letter, make the drop shadow light gray or some other light color. Don't use a shade that makes the letter look secondary.

Practice the techniques you've learned so far by making the New Year's sign shown here. What have you got to lose? Paper is cheap!

1. Lay out the letters using your normal handwriting.

2. Make corrections to the layout, then make the lines darker.

3. Try the brushwork. See how these letters break into the simple strokes we've been practicing? I added the connectors in the next step.

4. Now move the pounce pattern down and to the left and pounce again to create drop shadows.

5. Here drop shadows have been added just to the capital letters; note how three-dimensional they look.

1. Finish the layout, straightening the lines of the rough sketch with a pencil. All your mistakes can be made on the paper layout.

2. Slide the transfer paper under the layout.

3. After centering your layout, use your stylus to trace over the copy lines. Press lightly; the copy will transfer. Don't forget to put in the guidelines.

4. With the copy transferred, you can now make your brush-strokes within the letter lines.

Welcome

NEIGHBOR

Hint

A word written in all capital script letters does not read as well as a combination of upper- and lowercase script letters.

If all capital letters are required in your layout, stay with the casual bold upright version of the standard alphabet, not script. Although nothing is ironclad in lettering, some styles just look better when laid out with planned continuity. You will probably find it much easier to stroke all capital letters on your first attempt.

BELLMAN

Bellman

Spacing Your Letters

Mechanical Spacing

In mechanical spacing, the same amount of space is allowed for every letter, regardless of its width. The result is that narrow letters, like **i**, have more air space around them than wider letters, like **m** or **w**. Typewriters use mechanical spacing. The words **PUMPKIN PIE** at right are shown in mechanical spacing. In this case, even the air space between the letters is even.

However, mechanical spacing does not always work, especially as the size of the letters increase. Small letters, such as those produced by a typewriter, can be off in spacing and not be noticed. But as the letters are enlarged, the spacing stands out. We will use the word **VALUE** as an example. When written mechanically in a small size, as in the above line, the **V** does not seem to be far away from the rest of the letters. However, the space between the **V** and **A** and the **L** and **U** expands as the letters gets larger and it will begin to look as though the **V** is hanging by itself. There is also an abundance of air space after the **L**, since it is an open letter.

Suppose we change the word to **LAVENDER**. See how the mechanical spacing appears to leave the letter **L** hanging out all by itself?

PUMPKIN PIE

Example of Good Readability

Poorly-Spaced Letters

There is an abundance of space between the **V** and **A**, as well as the **L** and **U**. There is less space between the **U** and **E**.

LAVENDER

Mechanical Spacing

Air Spacing

We can, with handlettering, change the width of letters to allow the air space between letters to be approximately the same. This might be the most important part of good-looking lettering.

Since all letters are not the same width and height, there is no established rule for spacing your letters appropriately. The human eye sees what is correct and the brain comprehends what proper air space is.

Letters like **E, A, T, F, O, L** and **V** can be condensed or extended to fit an area. All letters can be heightened to fill vertical space.

The air space between each letter should be approximately the same. If the letters are spaced correctly, the sight of the word will be more pleasant. Open letters, such as **E, T, F** or **L**, automatically have more air space built-in. Those types of letters can then be placed closer to other letters for good readability.

Remember, the human eye sees good spacing.

In the air space examples at right, the space between the letters is almost the same, at least the way the human eye perceives it. However, some of the letters almost touch each other, such as the **L** and the **A**. The top of the letter **V** is almost exactly in a vertical line with the left downstroke of the letter **A**. That is what air space does. The word looks and reads completely at first sight.

VALUE

Properly Spaced Letters

LAVENDER

Mechanical Spacing Properly Adjusted for Good Air Space

Changing the Width and Height of Your Letters

We can shorten the width of letters like **A, O, T, E** and **F** to take up less space. Or we can widen any of those letters to use up more space between letters.

Hint

I am certain that most artists see the proper spacing of letters without paying much attention to the process, just as most see perspective in their drawings.

Surely all artists notice when perspective is off somewhat. Hopefully this display will help you pay attention to the spacing in your letters.

ETOLVA

ETOLVA

By condensing the width of letters, you can fit them in a smaller area.

VIOLET

VIOLET

Letters can also be widened to fill space.

Transferring Your Layout to a Project

1. Tape your layout or pattern over the surface, carefully placing it where the copy will go. Slide transfer paper under the layout. Press lightly with your stylus as you transfer your copy so as not to make indentations in the surface.

2. As you transfer your copy, you can lift up the transfer paper and pattern to see if you are in the correct place.

3. Now you can follow your lines and make the strokes necessary to complete the lettering.

Tricks of the Trade

When we teach a lettering seminar, the "zingers" that cause the most discussion and give the most enjoyment and sense of accomplishment are what we call the "tricks of the trade."

Every craft has shortcuts that are developed over time. Some are time-saving steps, others are ways to improve the look of the finished product, and some are systems that make the job easier. There are also tricks developed out of sheer necessity. Maybe a circle is needed when no template is available, or an oval must be enlarged.

The tricks we are presenting are going to help you design shapes for future projects. You may fine a good piece of wood in your garage, which, with a change of shape, could become a door plaque. Maybe you can paint and letter a mailbox with an address design you have wanted to do for years.

These tricks are not new and are very simply performed. You'll probably be surprised at how easy they are and wonder why you haven't thought of them before now. So let's get started.

We hope you enjoy them.

Drawing Straight Lines

Every project starts with straight lines. The horizon is a straight line. Boxes have straight lines. Circles start with straight lines, i.e., radius and diameter. Thank heaven for rulers.

All we need is a straight edge to draw a straight line, right? Well, we can draw a multitude of straight lines with or without a straight edge. And with a little planning, we can make all sizes of squares and rectangles.

Hint

Don't expect the first few lines you draw to be perfectly straight. But move the ruler up slightly each time you pull through with the pencil until you get the "feel" of both hands moving in unison. After a few pulls through, you'll notice how easy it is to draw straight lines without placing the ruler across the paper each time. Once again, the more you practice this move, the better the quality of your work will become. Our students must really get tired of us always repeating that word—practice, practice, practice. But this is the key to success.

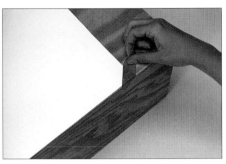

1. Let's start by laying a piece of paper down on a table and fastening it with tape at the four corners. Preferably, the bottom edge of the paper will be flush with the edge of the table. I find it easier to do the following moves if I turn my body slightly toward the left side since I am right-handed. My right side then is next to the table. I can then reach to the left side of the paper, allowing the freedom of movement needed to take the next step.

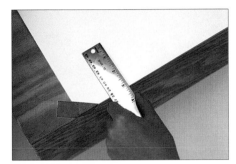

2. Put a ruler in your left hand if you are right-handed, vice versa if you are left-handed. Hold the ruler between your thumb and index finger, with maybe two inches or more lying flat on the table.

3. Using your thumbnail and the side of your index finger as a guide, place a pencil on the top edge of the ruler and pull the ruler and pencil together from the left edge of the paper to the right edge, pressing down with the pencil to draw the line.

4. Practice this move of making straight lines until you are comfortable with it. You will find it much easier than measuring several times across your copy area and connecting dots with a T-square or ruler.

Borders and Inset Lines

We can now show a way to create cleaner, better-looking borders and inset lines.

This next move is one that will require you to face more to the right (if you are right-handed), or at least have your project facing that way so that you can run your right hand from top to bottom or from right to left, as the case may be. Study the pictures carefully. This will help you in the future tremendously.

1. Hold the chalk or pencil between your index finger and your thumb.

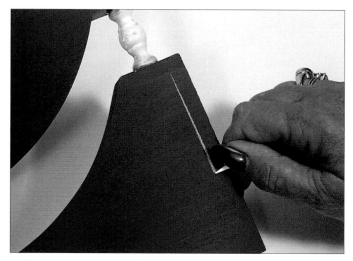

2. Place the remaining three fingertips so they rest on the edge of your project, or on the edge of the table upon which you are working. Run your hand down the edge, holding your thumb and finger as steady as possible. Start by making a line close to the edge of the table.

3. After you master this technique, try it with a liner brush in your hand. You will notice that as you develop control over the steadiness of the thumb and index finger, you will be able to make borders or inset lines around any shape. This same technique works equally well with a pencil or a loaded brush.

Circles

There are many traditional ways to draw circles. Protractors from high school geometry, coins (dimes, half dollars), plastic patterns available at art or school supply stores and adjustable compasses can do the job. But what if the circle is larger than these will do, or those tools are not available at the time? Let's have some fun and draw some circles. Shaping circles with a piece of paper is an easy way to get the size you want. And there are an infinite number of sizes you can get without making absolute measurements. If we could find paper long enough, we could make a circle the diameter of a football field. This is just so much fun!

1. Say the circle needed is 6 inches (15cm) in diameter. How can we do that easily? Consider using a piece of paper as the radius of the circle. Fold a sheet of paper at least 4 to 5 inches (10cm to 13cm) long lengthwise, in order to make the paper more rigid (or use lightweight cardboard).

2. Take a thumbtack or something similar and puncture a hole about half an inch (1.3cm) from one end. Puncture another hole 3 inches (7.5cm) along the paper from the first. If you don't have a ruler, a dollar bill is approximately 6 inches (15cm) long. Fold it in half.

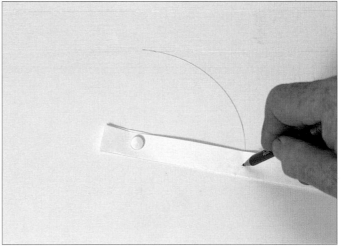

3. Place the thumbtack in the first hole, then place it in the center of the proposed circle. Insert the pencil point in the second hole. Now pull the pencil around in a circular motion until the circle is formed.

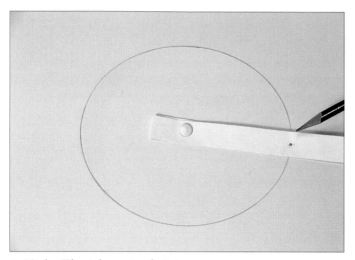

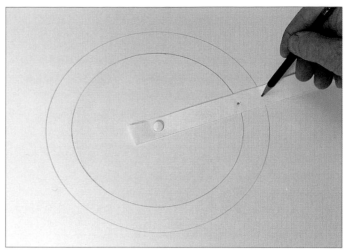

4. Viola! That's how simple it is.

By extending or decreasing the distance between the thumbtacks, we can make a circle any size we want.

Money Trick

Credit cards, by the way, are a little over 2 inches (5cm) high and almost 3 inches (7.5cm) wide. Standard typing paper is 8½″ × 11″ (22cm × 28cm). A quarter is 1 inch (2.5cm) in diameter. Pennies are ¾-inch (2cm) wide.

You can probably find many other standard items that have established sizes to help you determine distances. That's half the fun of decorative painting. There are plastic rulers that have various size holes and lines that can be used, but if that ruler is not available, what the heck!

Note how these standard items translate into measurements.

Checkerboards

Once a box is formed of any dimension, so long as it is square (i.e. 23″ × 23″ or 50cm × 50cm) we can divide it into any number of smaller boxes that are each square. This technique will work any time an area must be divided into equal sections, such as for a checkerboard. The more you use it, the more fun you will have.

1. We start the construction of a checkerboard by drawing out top and bottom lines long enough to allow for the division into smaller squares.

2. Measure the distance from the top line to the bottom line, then mark this same distance from left to right. We're using a 12-inch (30.5cm) square for this demonstration. Now the box is formed. Keep in mind that eight squares vertically and eight squares horizontally are required.

3. Place the ruler, or preferably a yardstick (1m ruler), on the paper layout. Put the top edge of the ruler on the top line. Angle the ruler until the 16 inch mark (40.6cm) is on the bottom line. Now make a light mark opposite the even numbered marks on the ruler, i.e., opposite the 2, 4, 6, 8, etc.

4. Make another series of light marks the same way further to the right. Using the straight line technique we practiced, or using a straightedge, draw the lines from the left edge of the box to the right, connecting the marks.

5. The same maneuver will now be used from the other sides by simply turning the paper, and repeating the exercise. What an easy way to measure! Measure the squares and you will find each checkerboard square is the same size, even though we did not have to measure each one.

Ovals

Surely we have all tried to form ovals of different sizes. Without a pattern of some sort it is almost impossible to draw an oval freehand. There is a simple way to do it, however, even though it may seem complicated at first.

Either a length of heavy-duty thread or a piece of thin picture-hanging wire will be needed for this procedure. We use these types of materials because they stretch less than ordinary string, making the finished product more exact.

Measure the approximate area to be covered by the oval on a piece of paper in order to make a pattern, which may be used to cut a piece of wood to your specifications. In that case we want to be "right on the money."

Play with this maneuver and experiment with different size ovals. You will never again have "horse collars" for ovals. Isn't this worth the price of admission alone?

With a little practice, it will now be possible to make any size oval needed, and it will be great fun to show this technique to someone who has never seen it.

1. Draw two lines approximately the size of the oval you wish to draw. Find the center.

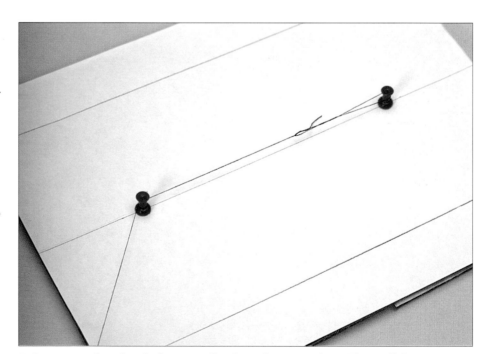

2. Insert two thumbtacks horizontally along the center line. This will determine the width of the oval. The length of the oval will be determined by how far out on the line the tacks are placed. Form a loop in the thread or wire, placing it over one thumbtack. Stretch the thread loosely and wrap the other end around the other tack. The amount of slack will then determine the height of the oval, so don't tie the second end. The amount of slack can be adjusted by increasing or decreasing the length of thread between the tacks.

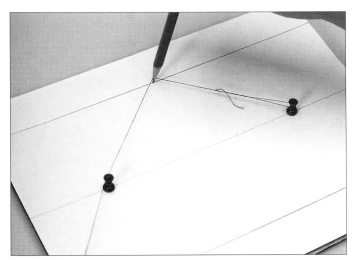

3. Using the tip of the pencil, push against the thread until it reaches the top limit of the top line.

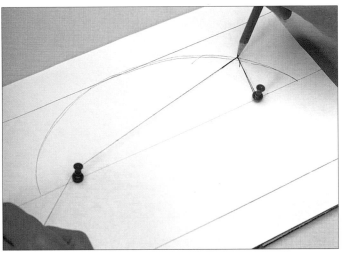

4. Press lightly with the pencil and pull the pencil toward one of the ends, keeping tension against the thread.

5. Proceed around the tack and toward the lower limit of the rectangle.

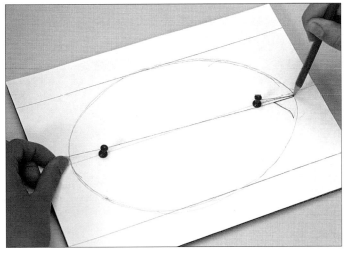

6. Continue along the bottom and up around the second tack, then to completion of the oval. You can now make ovals any size you want, just by moving the tacks.

You have now been exposed to our tricks of the trade. Pay close attention to the pictures available and develop your skills so that you can become speedier and more adept at completing your art projects.

You probably can already visualize your own uses for these ideas. We hope that you will use these techniques often and with great success.

From all the comments past students have made, I am sure that you will have much fun performing these simple tasks. You will probably want to show your friends. The more you practice, the better you will get.

Once again, practice, practice, practice! And remember, "act" is part of "practice."

Projects to Get You Started

These projects are intended to show you the many ways lettering can enhance your painted surfaces. They display not only various lettering styles, but linework, which is almost always used on my painted pieces. I like to call it "the finishing touch." Stretch your imagination and try different surfaces—from a small box to a signboard or piece of furniture. Go for it!

English Teas

When I saw this darling board I knew exactly what colors I'd use. I love blue, yellow and white together. This color scheme is very popular right now. There's lots of it in my house and this board will go in my kitchen. However, just because certain colors are trendy doesn't mean that you have to go with them. Try your favorite color combination and make your heart sing.

1. Sand and seal the board.
2. Base the entire board with Light Buttermilk. Base the grooves with Sapphire. Transfer the pattern.
3. Base the ribbon with Golden Straw, shade with Raw Sienna and Burnt Sienna, and highlight with Light Buttermilk and Titanium White.
4. Base the leaves with Hauser Medium Green, shade with Hauser Dark Green and highlight with Hauser Light Green and Golden Straw. Tint the leaves with Burgundy Wine.
5. Base the berries with Williamsburg Blue, shade with Deep Midnight Blue and highlight with Light Buttermilk. Add a dot highlight with Titanium White. Paint the blossom ends with Lamp Black.
6. Paint the linework with Sapphire. Paint the dots with Golden Straw.
7. Add the lettering with Sapphire.

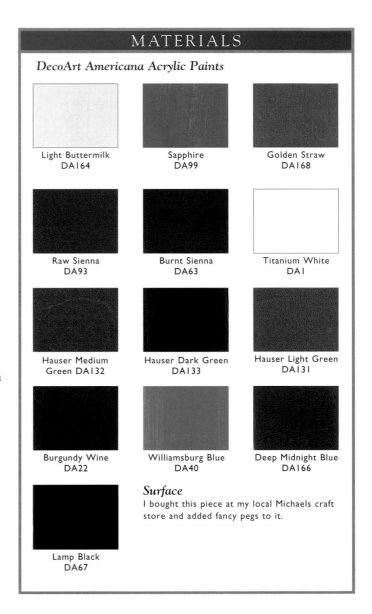

MATERIALS

DecoArt Americana Acrylic Paints

Light Buttermilk DA164

Sapphire DA99

Golden Straw DA168

Raw Sienna DA93

Burnt Sienna DA63

Titanium White DA1

Hauser Medium Green DA132

Hauser Dark Green DA133

Hauser Light Green DA131

Burgundy Wine DA22

Williamsburg Blue DA40

Deep Midnight Blue DA166

Lamp Black DA67

Surface
I bought this piece at my local Michaels craft store and added fancy pegs to it.

This pattern may be hand-traced or photocopied for personal use only. Enlarge at 167% on a photocopier to return to full size.

Eat, Drink and Be Merry

We thought this lazy Susan would be a good place to try your hand at making magic circles. You will make a large circle and several bands of color in varying widths. This creates a band to set in your lettering and gives you a chance to practice thick-and-thin brushstroke lettering as well as lettering on a curve.

Just think, when you are able to accomplish this project, you'll be able to attack that round kitchen table you have always wanted to paint.

1. Sand and seal the surface.
2. Base with Desert Sand.
3. To base your circle, mix Burgundy Wine plus Light Buttermilk to make a rich, rose color.
4. To create the marbled effect, dampen the surface with water. Pick up Burgundy Wine with a damp sea wool sponge. Pounce off the excess paint on your palette pad, then apply the remaining paint to the surface. Let dry.
5. Re-dampen the surface with water and repeat step 4, this time using Rookwood Red. Let dry.
6. Repeat step 4 with Light Buttermilk mixed with a touch of Burgundy Wine. Let dry.
7. Dampen the surface again. With a good liner brush, add some vein lines with Titanium White. While they are still wet, soften the veins with a damp sponge or mop brush.
8. Add the trim lines with Hauser Dark Green, and Burgundy Wine plus Rookwood Red.
9. Transfer the vine pattern. Paint the vines with a no. 2 liner and thinned Raw Sienna. Shade with Burnt Umber and highlight with Light Buttermilk.
10. Paint the leaves each in one stroke using Hauser Medium Green. Shade with a float of Hauser Dark Green and highlight with Celery Green.
11. Paint the little berries by dipping the handle end of a rather large-handled brush into Country Red. Hold the brush as vertically as possible and drop the dots off the end of the handle. Reload as necessary. When

dry, place a stroke of Black Plum on each berry for shading. Add a stroke of Burnt Orange on the opposite side for the highlight.
12. Paint the scrolls with Black Green, intertwining them over the twig.

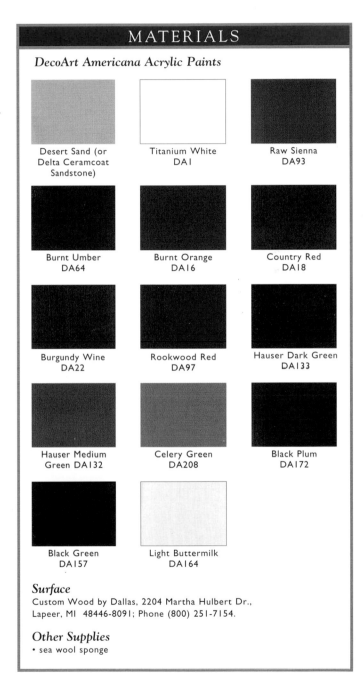

MATERIALS

DecoArt Americana Acrylic Paints

Desert Sand (or Delta Ceramcoat Sandstone)

Titanium White DA1

Raw Sienna DA93

Burnt Umber DA64

Burnt Orange DA16

Country Red DA18

Burgundy Wine DA22

Rookwood Red DA97

Hauser Dark Green DA133

Hauser Medium Green DA132

Celery Green DA208

Black Plum DA172

Black Green DA157

Light Buttermilk DA164

Surface
Custom Wood by Dallas, 2204 Martha Hulbert Dr., Lapeer, MI 48446-8091; Phone (800) 251-7154.

Other Supplies
• sea wool sponge

This pattern may be hand-traced or photocopied for personal use only. Enlarge at 134% on a photocopier to return to full size.

Miss American Pie

1. Sand and seal the piece.
2. Base the piece with Desert Sand.
3. To create the sponged effect, pick up some Rookwood Red on a damp sea wool sponge. Pounce off the excess paint on your palette pad. Apply the remaining paint to the sides of the basket with light pressure. Repeat until you have a nice, soft look.
4. Pick up Burgundy Wine and repeat step 3. If the sponging looks too solid, you can always sponge back over it with your base color.
5. Base the handle supports with Rookwood Red.
6. When dry, wash over them with Burgundy Wine.
7. Stain the three-dimensional apple on the lid and the crossbar handle with Burgundy Wine.
8. Paint the linework with Burgundy Wine plus Rookwood Red.
9. Paint the lettering with Hauser Dark Green.
10. Transfer the fruit pattern. Base the plums with Pansy Lavender. Shade with Dioxazine Purple. Highlight with Pansy Lavender mixed with Light Buttermilk, then just Light Buttermilk. Wash over the plums with Burgundy Wine or add Burgundy Wine tints. Repeat the highlight.
11. Base the cherries with Cherry Red. Shade with Dioxazine Purple plus Burgundy Wine. Highlight with a wash of Napthol Red plus Golden Straw. Let dry, then drybrush sparingly with Cadmium Yellow. Streak the stem shadow in with a bit of Cadmium Yellow. Paint the stem with Burnt Sienna. Shade the stem with Burnt Umber and highlight with Light Buttermilk.
12. Base the apples with Celery Green. Deepen the dark sides with Celery Green plus Plantation Pine, then a bit of straight Plantation Pine. Keep the apple streaky. Drybrush with Cadmium Yellow for the highlight.
13. Base the pears with Golden Straw. Shade with Raw Sienna, then Burnt Sienna plus Napthol Red. Tint with a wash of Burgundy Wine. Spatter the pears with Burnt Sienna.

MATERIALS

DecoArt Americana Acrylic Paints

Pansy Lavender DA154

Dioxazine Purple DA101

Cherry Red DA159

Napthol Red DA104

Plantation Pine DA113

Hauser Dark Green DA133

Celery Green DA208

Cadmium Yellow DA10

Burgundy Wine DA22

Rookwood Red DA97

Burnt Sienna DA63

Burnt Umber DA64

Golden Straw DA168

Raw Sienna DA93

Desert Sand (or Delta Ceramcoat Sandstone)

Light Buttermilk DA164

Surface
Fred's Frames and Woodworks
3807 Seiler Rd.
Dorsey, IL 62021
Phone: (618) 377-3200

Other Supplies
• sea wool sponge

14. Base the leaves with Celery Green. Shade with Plantation Pine. Highlight with a dry brush and Cadmium Yellow. Tint with other colors from this project.
15. Spatter the empty corners of the inner square and the fruit lightly with thinned Burnt Sienna. Varnish.

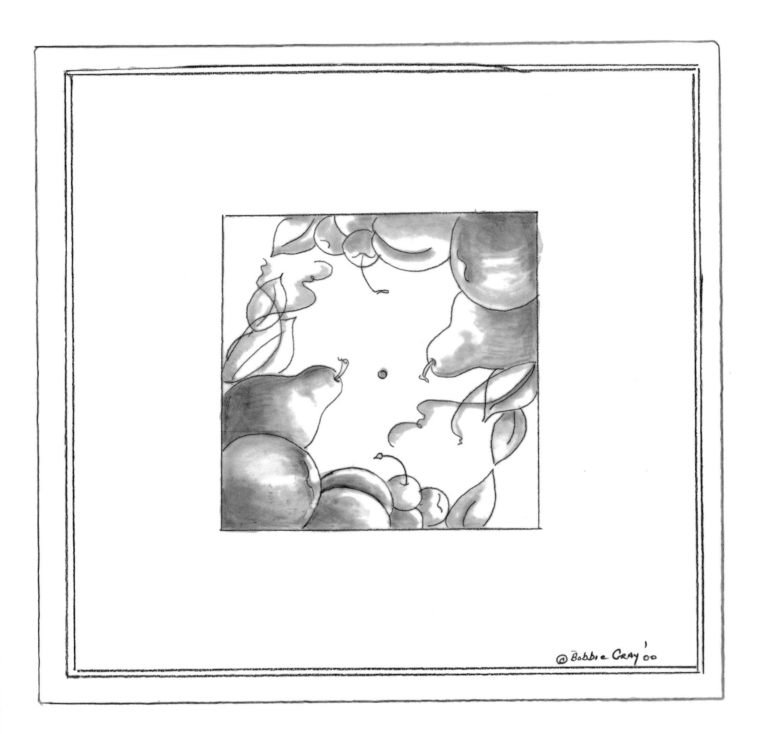

@ Bobbie Gray '00

This pattern may be hand-traced or photocopied for personal use only. Enlarge at 159% on a photocopier to return to full size. This pattern is for project three, beginning on page 90.

Love Makes a Happy Home

Love Makes a Happy Home

1. Sand and seal the board.

2. Base the board with Williamsburg Blue and the frame with Williamsburg Blue plus Deep Midnight Blue.

3. Paint the clouds with Light Buttermilk.

4. Paint the house with Georgia Clay grayed down with a touch of Williamsburg Blue. Paint the roof and windows with Country Blue plus Titanium White and shade with Deep Midnight Blue. Shade the house with Rookwood Red. Add bricks here and there with Rookwood Red. Paint the trimwork with Light Buttermilk or Titanium White.

5. Paint the trunks of the trees by the house Raw Sienna and shade with Burnt Sienna, then Burnt Umber. Highlight with Raw Sienna plus Light Buttermilk, then just Light Buttermilk.

6. Stipple the foliage using Hauser Medium Green; let some sky show through. Shade the foliage with Hauser Dark Green, still allowing the sky to show. Highlight with Hauser Light Green. Accent with some touches of Golden Straw and maybe a bit of Light Buttermilk.

7. Paint the low hedges with Hauser Dark Green, then Hauser Medium Green and finally Hauser Light Green.

8. Stipple the evergreen trees with Hauser Medium Green. Shade the outside edge with Hauser Dark Green. Highlight with Hauser Light Green plus a touch of Golden Straw.

9. Using a no. 4 liner, make the stems and leaves for all of the flowers with Hauser Medium Green, then shade with Hauser Dark Green and highlight with Hauser Light Green. All of the flowers are basically painted the same way. Create the leaves and flowers by tapping in the color very loosely with the liner. Make each color of flower a different height and width, from tall and straight to low and spreading. How you arrange the colors is up to you.

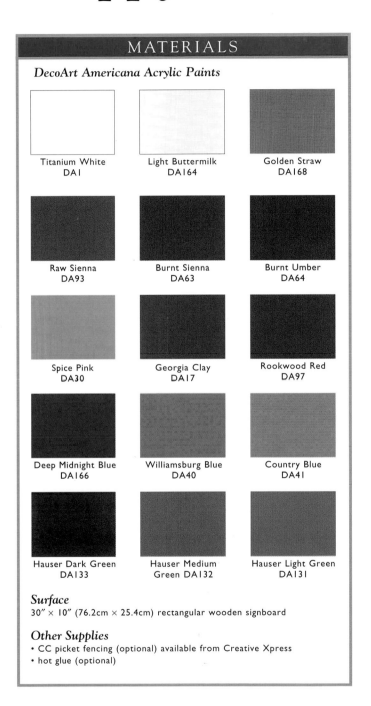

MATERIALS

DecoArt Americana Acrylic Paints

Titanium White DA1

Light Buttermilk DA164

Golden Straw DA168

Raw Sienna DA93

Burnt Sienna DA63

Burnt Umber DA64

Spice Pink DA30

Georgia Clay DA17

Rookwood Red DA97

Deep Midnight Blue DA166

Williamsburg Blue DA40

Country Blue DA41

Hauser Dark Green DA133

Hauser Medium Green DA132

Hauser Light Green DA131

Surface
30" × 10" (76.2cm × 25.4cm) rectangular wooden signboard

Other Supplies
• CC picket fencing (optional) available from Creative Xpress
• hot glue (optional)

- Base the blue flowers with Country Blue plus Light Buttermilk. Shade with Deep Midnight Blue and highlight with Titanium White.
- Base the pink flowers with Spice Pink plus Light Buttermilk. Shade with Rookwood Red and highlight with Titanium White.
- Base the yellow flowers with Golden Straw. Shade with Raw Sienna and highlight with Titanium White.
10. Paint the birdhouse pole with Raw Sienna, shade with Burnt Sienna and Burnt Umber and highlight with Raw Sienna, then Light Buttermilk.
11. Paint the lettering with Titanium White.
12. You can paint a white picket fence across the bottom of the board up to the edge of the house, or hot glue miniature picket fencing to the board. You can even pull some of your flowers out onto the pickets. Be creative.

This pattern may be hand-traced or photocopied for personal use only. Reattach the two halves and enlarge at 200% on a photocopier to return to full size.

Nana's Kitchen

The lettering on this board reinforces the shape of the oval, but the strokes that make up the letters are the same basic brushstrokes you've learned. It's always fun to try something different, so jump right in and get started.

1. Sand and seal the board.
2. Base the board with Light Buttermilk. Let dry.
3. Apply a checkerboard pattern using a checkerboard or square stencil and Golden Straw.
4. Lightly transfer the pattern from pages 98–99.
5. Base the pitcher with a thin wash of Payne's Grey. Float thinned Payne's Grey around the shape of the pitcher, then fill the opening with the same mix. Deepen the shaded areas on the pitcher with floats of Payne's Grey. Add the stripes with Golden Straw. Shade the edges of the pitcher with Burnt Sienna. Add a thin, wavy band of Sapphire plus Titanium White. Repeat the floats of Payne's Grey around the pitcher. Add Titanium White highlights.
6. Float Payne's Grey plus a touch of Sapphire around the shape of the little spattered crock. Dampen the crock with clean water; it should be pretty wet. With a liner, make squiggles with Titanium White, Sapphire and a touch of Payne's Gray, then blot with a paper towel. Do this several times until you achieve the right look. Darken the shaded area of the crock with Payne's Grey. Add a white highlight to the crock. Define the rim with Titanium White, Sapphire and Payne's Grey.
7. Paint the spoon with a wash of Titanium White and Sapphire and shade with Payne's Grey.
8. Wash over the bottom of the cupcakes with Raw Sienna and shade with Burnt Sienna. Add icing with Titanium White and shade this area softly with Payne's Grey. Add a Titanium White highlight to the top of the cupcakes.
9. Wash over the cheesecake with thinned Raw Sienna. Shade with Raw Sienna and Burnt Sienna, then add a Titanium White highlight. Paint the plate

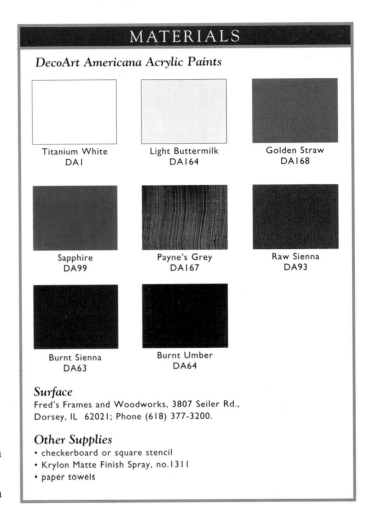

MATERIALS

DecoArt Americana Acrylic Paints

Titanium White
DA1

Light Buttermilk
DA164

Golden Straw
DA168

Sapphire
DA99

Payne's Grey
DA167

Raw Sienna
DA93

Burnt Sienna
DA63

Burnt Umber
DA64

Surface
Fred's Frames and Woodworks, 3807 Seiler Rd., Dorsey, IL 62021; Phone (618) 377-3200.

Other Supplies
• checkerboard or square stencil
• Krylon Matte Finish Spray, no.1311
• paper towels

Titanium White with a touch of Sapphire, and shade with Sapphire.

10. Wash in the metal pot and spoon with thinned Payne's Grey. Shade with full-strength Payne's Grey and add a white highlight. Shade the inside of the pot with thinned Payne's Grey, Titanium White and Sapphire.
11. Wash in the pie with thinned Raw Sienna. Shade with Raw Sienna plus Burnt Sienna and add a Titanium White highlight. Paint the pan with Sapphire plus a touch of Titanium White. Shade the pan with Sapphire plus a touch of Payne's Grey.
12. Wash in the cabinet with Raw Sienna. Shade with Raw Sienna, then Burnt Sienna, then Burnt Umber.

Add the detail lines with thinned Burnt Umber and a liner brush. Highlight the cabinet with Light Buttermilk, then Titanium White.

13. I usually spray the surface lightly with Krylon Matte Finish Spray, no. 1311, if I'm going to spatter it. That way, if I don't like the effect, I can wipe it off. Spatter the design with thinned Sapphire, using your no. 6 liner.

14. Apply the lettering with Sapphire and a no. 6 liner.

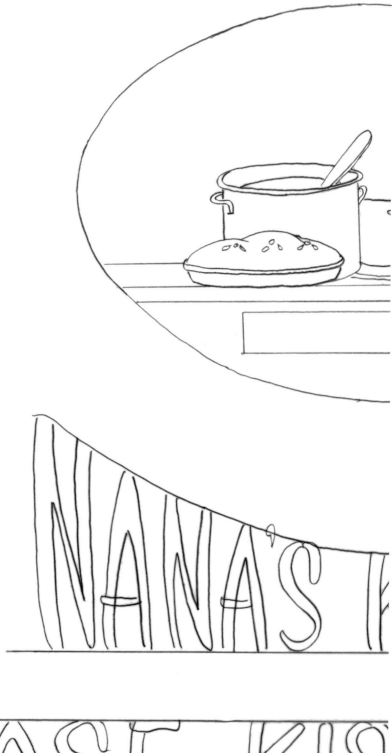

This pattern may be hand-traced or photocopied for personal use only. Reattach the two halves and enlarge at 134% on a photocopier to return to full size.

Christmas Is Here

I paint Christmas items all year long. When I finished this painting, there was some negative area left and the words to this song kept running through my head, so I lettered them on the painting. This is one of my favorite pieces.

1. Sand and seal the surface.
2. Base the panel with two coats of Black Green.
3. Apply the pattern. Wash the cabinet top and bottom with a mix of Black Green plus Hauser Medium Green about two values lighter than the background. Paint the wood grain lines with Lamp Black.
4. Base the candle, berries and top of the reindeer stand with Country Red.
5. Base the candle base with Golden Straw.
6. Base the reindeer with a medium value gray made from Lamp Black plus Titanium White.
7. Base some of the leaves with Hauser Medium Green and some with Hauser Medium Green plus Hauser Dark Green.
8. Shade all of the leaves with Hauser Dark Green. Deepen the shading with Hauser Dark Green plus Black Green. Highlight the lighter leaves with Hauser Light Green. Highlight the other leaves with Hauser Light Green plus Hauser Medium Green. Add Country Blue tints to the darkest leaves and Burgundy Wine tints to the lighter leaves. Paint the leaf veins with Hauser Medium Green, shade with Black Green and highlight with Celery Green.
9. Shade the candle with Burgundy Wine, then deepen with floats of Black Plum plus a tad of Burgundy Wine. Shade the darkest areas with Black Plum. Add wax drips with Country Red plus Burnt Orange. Shade the drips with Black Plum and highlight with Burnt Orange, then Burnt Orange plus Light Buttermilk. Base the wick with the medium gray mix from step 6. Crosshatch the wick with Lamp Black and highlight with Light Buttermilk.
10. Keep the flame transparent. Place Burnt Orange in the flame shape. Add a streak of Golden Straw to the right side, and a Country Blue streak to the left side.

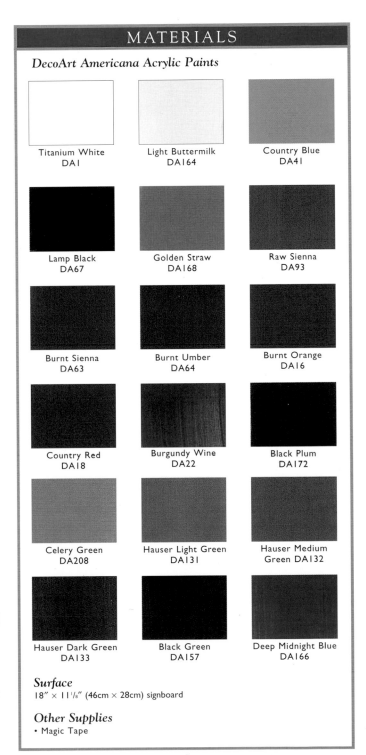

MATERIALS

DecoArt Americana Acrylic Paints

Titanium White
DA1

Light Buttermilk
DA164

Country Blue
DA41

Lamp Black
DA67

Golden Straw
DA168

Raw Sienna
DA93

Burnt Sienna
DA63

Burnt Umber
DA64

Burnt Orange
DA16

Country Red
DA18

Burgundy Wine
DA22

Black Plum
DA172

Celery Green
DA208

Hauser Light Green
DA131

Hauser Medium
Green DA132

Hauser Dark Green
DA133

Black Green
DA157

Deep Midnight Blue
DA166

Surface
18" × 11⅛" (46cm × 28cm) signboard

Other Supplies
• Magic Tape

Wash a little Country Red over the orange.

11. Shade the outside edges of the candle base with Raw Sienna. Walk this color toward the middle. Next, shade with Burnt Sienna. Walk this color in, but not as far as the first float. Drag the chisel edge of the brush into the creases. Darken the shading with Burnt Umber plus Black Green. Highlight the middle area of the candle base with Golden Straw plus Light Buttermilk, then Light Buttermilk plus a touch of Titanium White.

12. Lay a piece of Magic Tape along the top of the lamp to help keep this line straight. Dampen the candle globe area with clean water. With a ¼-inch (2cm) brush, float the gray mix down the sides. Add a line across the top, then remove the tape. Add tints of Country Red and some Burnt Orange to the globe near the leaves. Add the highlight with Light Buttermilk, then Titanium White.

13. Shade the reindeer with a darker value of the gray mix (more Lamp Black). Tint with touches of Country Red and Burnt Orange. Highlight with Light Buttermilk. Shade the top of the stand with Black Plum, then Black Plum plus Black Green. Paint the next section of the stand with Hauser Medium Green. Shade with Hauser Dark Green, then Hauser Dark Green plus Black Green. Highlight the center with Hauser Medium Green and Light Buttermilk, then just Light Buttermilk.

14. Base the blocks with Raw Sienna plus Burnt Umber. Add squares of Country Red and outline with Lamp Black. Paint the letters on

the block with Raw Sienna plus Golden Straw.

15. Base the star with Golden Straw. Set a line ⅛ inch (3mm) in from the edge of the star. Float Burnt Sienna against this line, and deepen with Burnt Umber. Shade the star where it is behind the ball ornament with Raw Sienna, then Burnt Sienna. Deepen further with Burnt Umber plus a tad of Black Green. Keep this color soft. Drybrush the center of the star with Light Buttermilk.

16. Base the crock with a dark gray mix and shade with dark gray plus Lamp Black. Shade the darkest areas with Burnt Umber. You will have to repeat this application to get it nice and dark. Paint the crack in the crock with the shading mixes. Add tints of Burgundy Wine to the sides of the crock and the rim. Add a wash of Country Blue to the right side of the crock, but not on the edge. Drybrush Light Buttermilk in the center of the crock. Spatter the crock with thin Burnt Umber plus Lamp Black.

17. Paint the ball ornament with the same colors as the crock.

s is Here

© BOBBIE GRAY '00

ROUTED EDGE

Drybrush the highlight after shading with Light Buttermilk.

18. Base the candy canes with Light Buttermilk. Paint the stripes with Country Red. Shade the inside of the curves with floats of Deep Midnight Blue. Shade to the left on the straight sections. Highlight with a line of Titanium White on the upper part of the candy canes.

19. Paint the twigs with Raw Sienna and shade with Burnt Umber, then Lamp Black. Highlight with Light Buttermilk.

20. Drybrush around the candle flame and outside the globe where it curves with very soft Golden Straw.

21. Paint the lettering with Country Red.

22. This might sound scary, but when I was all through with the painting I took a 1-inch (2.5cm) flat brush and very watered-down Black Green and washed over the whole panel to add an instant antiqued look and soften everything down. This wash must be very transparent. Do not do this more than two times. When dry, varnish your favorite way.

Angels Abide

I believe in angels and hope you do, too. Let this little angel keep watch over you.

This is an illustration of thick-and-thin lettering, my favorite, and a little tricky linework. Linework doesn't always have to completely encompass your lettering. Add some dots and "pudmuckles" at the end of your broken linework.

I modified the original surface, which was a 13″ × 7⅛″ (33cm × 18cm) rectangle, by cutting the bottom piece from the top and then reattaching the pieces with wooden pegs. I cut the ends off the pegs and used a heavy-duty wood glue for this purpose. You could also leave the ends on the pegs and drill holes in the two pieces for the pegs to fit into. The finished dimensions of the modified piece are 13″ × 8½″ (33cm × 22cm).

1. Sand and seal the surface.
2. Apply a coat of thinned Light Buttermilk to the board and wipe off the excess while still wet. The grain of the wood should show through. If this application isn't heavy enough, repeat the process.
3. Apply the pattern lightly.
4. Add the lettering with Rookwood Red.
5. Trim the edge of the boards and paint the inset lines with Rookwood Red.
6. Base the angel's halo with Glorious Gold. Paint the dots and inside line with Deep Midnight Blue. Paint the outside line with Rookwood Red.
7. Base the face with Flesh Tone, easing the color up into the hair area.
8. Fill the eye sockets with Titanium White. Place the eyeball with Salem Blue plus Deep Midnight Blue. Paint the pupil Lamp Black. Float Lamp Black across the top of the whole eye to set it back. Outline the eye lightly with Lamp Black. Float Salem Blue very softly above the eyes. Add the eyelid with a stroke of Lamp Black plus a tad of Raw Sienna. Paint the eyebrows with Raw Sienna. Paint the lashes Lamp Black. Add Titanium White highlights and a glim-

mer of Glorious Gold in the pupils.

9. Dampen the cheeks with clean water. While wet, softly float with Country Red.
10. Float above the nose with a pale mix of Country Red plus Titanium White. The nose is a half circle of Raw Sienna with a Titanium White highlight.
11. Paint the lips with Country Red plus Flesh Tone. Paint the opening in the mouth with Rookwood Red. Deepen the left side with Rookwood Red plus Lamp Black.

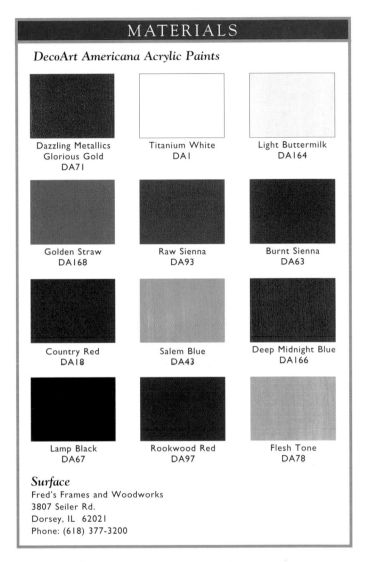

MATERIALS

DecoArt Americana Acrylic Paints

Dazzling Metallics Glorious Gold DA71	Titanium White DA1	Light Buttermilk DA164
Golden Straw DA168	Raw Sienna DA93	Burnt Sienna DA63
Country Red DA18	Salem Blue DA43	Deep Midnight Blue DA166
Lamp Black DA67	Rookwood Red DA97	Flesh Tone DA78

Surface
Fred's Frames and Woodworks
3807 Seiler Rd.
Dorsey, IL 62021
Phone: (618) 377-3200

12. Float the outside edges of the wings with Salem Blue plus Light Buttermilk. Add an outline of the same mix. Add easy comma strokes at the tops of the wings. Protect the face with a scrap of paper and spatter the wings softly with Salem Blue.

13. With a good liner, add hair squiggles with Rookwood Red, then Burnt Sienna, then Golden Straw. Highlight with Titanium White, then add a few Glorious Gold highlights.

14. Base the dress with Rookwood Red. Shade under the collar and down the center of the dress with Rookwood Red plus Lamp Black. Paint the collar with Salem Blue plus Light Buttermilk. Outline the top and bottom of the collar and the bottom of the dress with Glorious Gold.

15. Spatter the board lightly with Rookwood Red, again protecting the face with a scrap of paper. Varnish and enjoy!

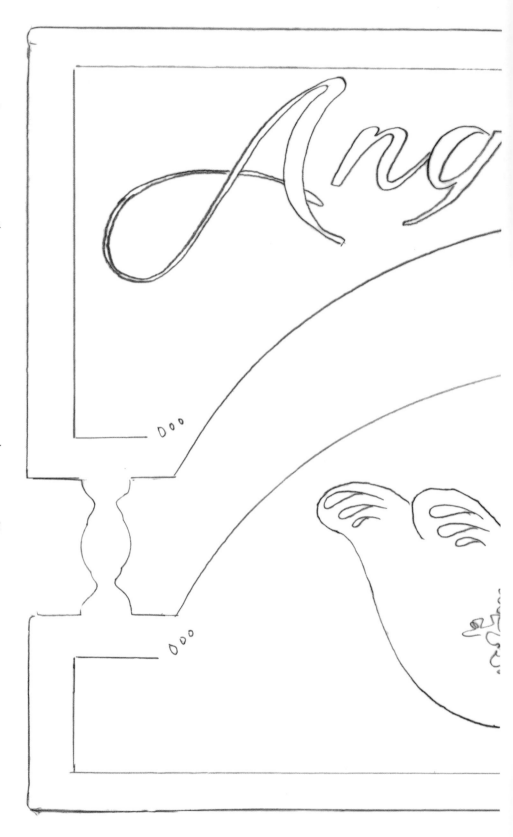

els Abide

© Bobbie Gray '98

This pattern may be hand-traced or photocopied for personal use only. Reattach the two halves and enlarge at 105% on a photocopier to return to full size.

Tulips

1. Sand and seal the board.

2. Basecoat the wood with Desert Sand.

3. With a ¾-inch (2cm) flat, slip-slap a very thin wash of Celery Green under the pattern area and a bit past the edge of the pattern. Darken the center of the pattern with a bit of Hauser Medium Green. Let dry.

4. You may now apply the pattern lightly. This is a very loosely-drawn design—you may add more leaves or flowers if you like.

5. Fill in the leaves with soft washes of Celery Green; also make some with Hauser Medium Green. Keep the lighter-value leaves to the outside of the pattern. Shade with floats of Hauser Medium Green and a bit of Deep Midnight Blue. Highlight with Golden Straw. Loosely outline the leaves with a "hit-and-miss" stroke of Hauser Medium Green and maybe a little Deep Midnight Blue.

6. With a no. 6 liner, pity-pat (tap the tip of the brush on the surface lightly and quickly) very thin Celery Green where you want the yellow background flowers to be. While still wet, add some pity-pats of Golden Straw. Keep the color soft and work a small area at a time. Highlight with pity-pats of Light Buttermilk. When you finish the tulips, you may want to pull some of these filler flowers over the tulip bottoms.

7. Base the blue tulip with Winter Blue. Shade with soft floated washes of Country Blue, then Deep Midnight Blue. Highlight with Light Buttermilk, then Titanium White. Add Deep Midnight Blue linework and outline each section of the tulip loosely with Deep Midnight Blue. Tint with Burgundy Wine plus Peony Pink.

8. Base the pink tulip with Peony Pink. Shade with soft floated washes of Burgundy Wine, then Burgundy Wine plus a tad of Deep Midnight Blue. Highlight with floats of Light Buttermilk, then Titanium White. Outline each section and do the linework

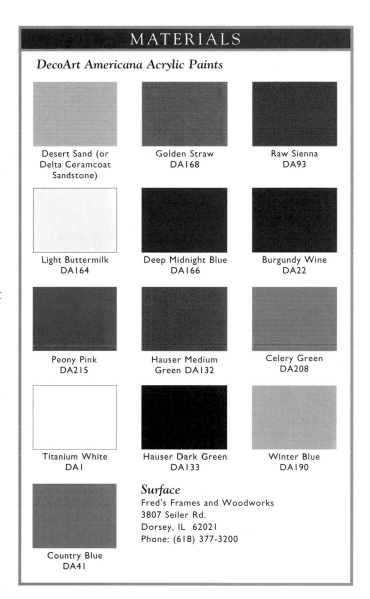

MATERIALS

DecoArt Americana Acrylic Paints

Desert Sand (or Delta Ceramcoat Sandstone)

Golden Straw DA168

Raw Sienna DA93

Light Buttermilk DA164

Deep Midnight Blue DA166

Burgundy Wine DA22

Peony Pink DA215

Hauser Medium Green DA132

Celery Green DA208

Titanium White DA1

Hauser Dark Green DA133

Winter Blue DA190

Country Blue DA41

Surface

Fred's Frames and Woodworks
3807 Seiler Rd.
Dorsey, IL 62021
Phone: (618) 377-3200

with Burgundy Wine.

9. Base the yellow tulip with Golden Straw. Shade with soft floated washes of Raw Sienna, then Raw Sienna plus Burgundy Wine. Paint the linework with Raw Sienna plus Burgundy Wine.

10. Add a white comma stroke to the main tip of each tulip.

11. Add touch-down strokes of Celery Green to the outside edges of the pattern. Also add some Hauser Dark Green vines. Shade inside the curves of your vines with Hauser Medium Green.

12. Add a Celery Green outline set in from the edge of the surface. Shade against the inside of the line with a float of Celery Green. Paint stripes outside the inset line with Country Blue plus a tad of Titanium White. Between each stripe, add a touch-down of Peony Pink using a no. 6 liner or a small filbert.

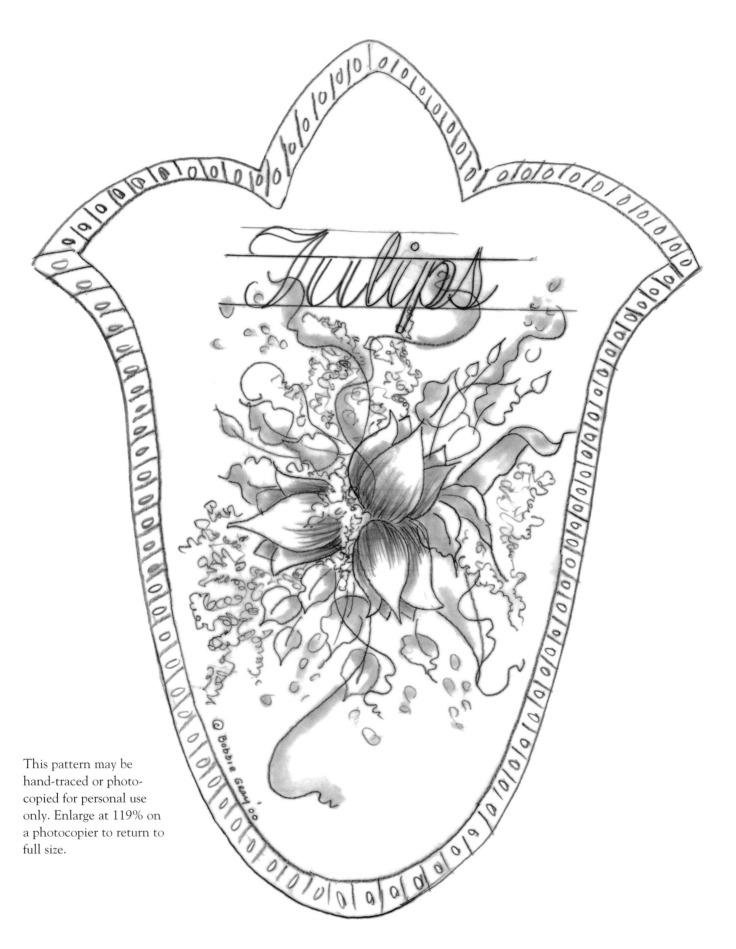

This pattern may be hand-traced or photo-copied for personal use only. Enlarge at 119% on a photocopier to return to full size.

© Bobbie Geary '00

Home Sweet Home

1. Sand and seal the surface.
2. Base the box with Light Buttermilk. Paint the handles and inside of the box Winter Blue. Apply the pattern.
3. Create the sky by streaking thinned Winter Blue across the Light Buttermilk background. Create some fluffy clouds with Titanium White plus a tad of Winter Blue. Deepen a bit under the clouds with a tad of Deep Midnight Blue.
4. Paint the hills with Hauser Medium Green. Shade with Hauser Dark Green. Highlight with Hauser Light Green.
5. Wash the grass with Hauser Light Green. Shade along the path and at the bottom with Hauser Medium Green.
6. Base the house with Golden Straw. Shade with Golden Straw plus Country Red. Also shade inside the door and windows with this mix, and use it to paint the bricks and steps. Trim around the windows and door with Titanium White. Paint the shutters with Hauser Light Green. Line the shutters with Hauser Medium Green. Lightly outline the steps with Burnt Umber.
7. Base the roof and chimney with Country Red. Shade with a float of Golden Straw plus Country Red, then add the linework to the edge with this mix. Drybrush Light Buttermilk in the center of the roof.
8. Base the banner with Golden Straw. Shade the tips with Country Red plus Golden Straw. Repeat this several times. Drybrush the center with Light Buttermilk.
9. Add Lamp Black detailing to the rooftop.
10. Shade the edges of the path with Raw Sienna, then Burnt Sienna.
11. Pull up Hauser Medium Green plus Hauser Dark Green stems for the blue flowers closest to the house. With your liner, add touches of Deep Midnight Blue, Winter Blue and Titanium White. Float Hauser Dark Green on the grass alongside the path. Pity-pat

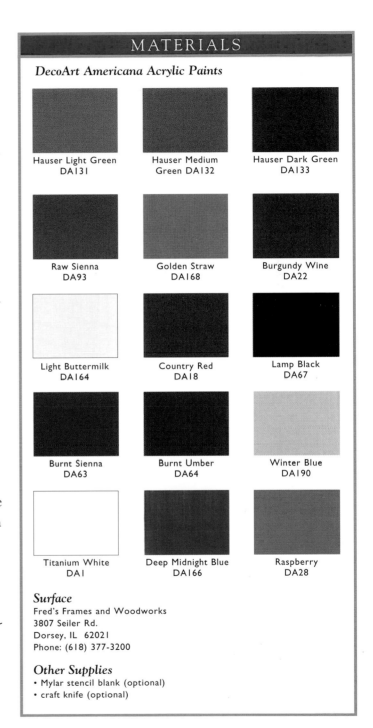

MATERIALS

DecoArt Americana Acrylic Paints

Hauser Light Green
DA131

Hauser Medium
Green DA132

Hauser Dark Green
DA133

Raw Sienna
DA93

Golden Straw
DA168

Burgundy Wine
DA22

Light Buttermilk
DA164

Country Red
DA18

Lamp Black
DA67

Burnt Sienna
DA63

Burnt Umber
DA64

Winter Blue
DA190

Titanium White
DA1

Deep Midnight Blue
DA166

Raspberry
DA28

Surface
Fred's Frames and Woodworks
3807 Seiler Rd.
Dorsey, IL 62021
Phone: (618) 377-3200

Other Supplies
• Mylar stencil blank (optional)
• craft knife (optional)

Hauser Medium Green and Hauser Dark Green along this area, then add touches of Golden Straw, Country Red and Titanium White for the tiny flowers. Paint the flowers on the lawn just as you did those closest to the house, only make them a little bigger.

12. I cut a stencil from Mylar to keep my trees the same size and neatly shaped. Lay the stencil where you want it, hold securely and stipple Hauser Medium Green lightly into the shape. Add Hauser Dark Green to the outside edges and Hauser Light Green to the inside edges. Work quickly, wet-into-wet. Paint the trunks with Raw Sienna and shade with Burnt Sienna, then Burnt Umber. Paint the pots with Raw Sienna and shade with Burnt Sienna, then Burnt Umber. Paint the pot rims with Raw Sienna plus Titanium White. Paint the insides of the pots with Burnt Umber.

13. Paint the lettering in the banner with the Country Red/Golden Straw mix.

14. Paint the stripes and the box outside the design with Golden Straw.

15. Paint the linework outlining the banner, the stripes and the box around the design with Raspberry.

16. Paint the vines on the stripes with Hauser Medium Green. Shade here and there with Hauser Dark Green.

17. Paint the rose leaves with Hauser Medium Green and shade with Hauser Dark Green. To paint the roses, load a no. 2 or no. 4 liner with Raspberry plus a tad of Burgundy Wine. Tip into Light Buttermilk and swirl the brush in a spiral on the surface. Add a few individual petals to the edges if you like.

18. Repeat the stripe design on the sides if you like. The main pattern could also be repeated on the back.

This pattern may be hand-traced or photocopied for personal use only. Reattach the two halves. The pattern is shown full size.

Welcome

Welcome

1. Sand and seal the board.
2. Base the board with Light Buttermilk. Trim with Winter Blue. Transfer the pattern.
3. Slip-slap the following colors on the basket with a ¾-inch (2cm) flat brush. Refer to the picture on page 116 for placement. Keep these colors transparent. Slip-slap Toffee and Mocha into the light areas of the basket. Slip-slap Light Buttermilk on the middle and the bulge of the basket. Softly float Sable Brown under the basket rim and slip-slap it into the dark areas of the basket. Casually tuck this color in between the weaves on the basket rim. I didn't pay too much attention to the actual weave of the basket; it is just suggested with dark and light values. Wash Sable Brown into the rest of the basket, keeping it soft. Shade between the horizontal wicker in the middle of the basket and in the areas to the left of that, first with Mocha, then with Khaki Tan. (Don't sweat this, this basket is very old and has been repaired.) Build your darks from Cashmere Beige to Burnt Umber or even Lamp Black, referring to the photo for help. Fill the ribbing on the basket rim and in the middle with Light Buttermilk and work over it with your darks; this is the only area I really detailed on the basket. The rest of the weave is created by shading darks against the weave lines and highlighting the center of the weave. I did very little "over and under." Use as many of the brown shades shown above as you like. Keep a casual approach, and just keep working with soft washes and floats. The handle also has most of the browns in it

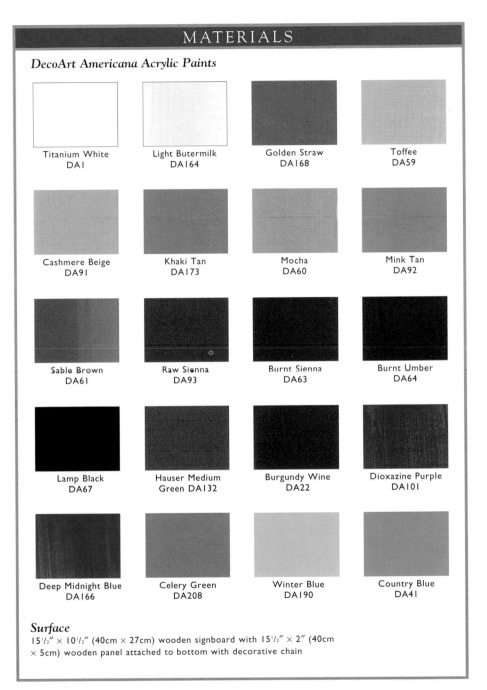

MATERIALS

DecoArt Americana Acrylic Paints

Titanium White DA1

Light Buttermilk DA164

Golden Straw DA168

Toffee DA59

Cashmere Beige DA91

Khaki Tan DA173

Mocha DA60

Mink Tan DA92

Sable Brown DA61

Raw Sienna DA93

Burnt Sienna DA63

Burnt Umber DA64

Lamp Black DA67

Hauser Medium Green DA132

Burgundy Wine DA22

Dioxazine Purple DA101

Deep Midnight Blue DA166

Celery Green DA208

Winter Blue DA190

Country Blue DA41

Surface
15½" × 10½" (40cm × 27cm) wooden signboard with 15½" × 2" (40cm × 5cm) wooden panel attached to bottom with decorative chain

and is streaked with the darker values and shaded with Burnt Umber, then Burnt Umber plus Lamp Black. Drybrush the final highlights on the basket with Light Buttermilk.

4. Slip-slap some of your greens in the flower area. Extend upward under the handle. You can also mix Raw Sienna plus Burgundy Wine and place this under the basket on the left and inside the basket where the flowers will extend. Mix Dioxazine Purple plus Mocha very transparently and extend this color where the flowers will fall on the right. Also use this mix and Burgundy Wine plus Mocha to make soft background leaves. You can soften the edges of your slip-slap strokes as you work with a damp, soft paper towel.

5. Trace the flower shapes on. Paint the leaves with one stroke each. I set mine outside the basket and added stems and curlicues using soft colors. I made more green leaves in the center of the basket using a no. 10 filbert loaded with a wash of Celery Green and then side loaded with a Hauser Medium Green wash. Paint the pale blue leaves with a wash of Winter Blue plus a tad of very thin, transparent Deep Midnight Blue. Paint the pink leaves with Burgundy Wine plus a tad of Dioxazine Purple or Deep Midnight Blue. Keep this very, very soft. Paint the stems with combinations of the above colors or Celery Green plus the above colors. Have fun with the leaves and use colors from your palette. When you have done all the flowers,

you may want to add more leaves—it's up to you.

6. Use a no. 6 round to paint the lilacs. Start by softly pity-patting a brush mix of Burgundy Wine plus Dioxazine Purple on the surface. Brush mixing will give you more variety. This is your darkest value; follow the shape of the flower. Next pity-pat a pink brush mix of Burgundy Wine plus Mocha. Create a few four-petaled florets here and there. Next pity-pat Burgundy Wine plus Mocha plus Titanium White. This is your lightest color. Make several four-petal florets with this mix. Add a Golden Straw dot to the centers of the four-petal florets.

7. Use a no. 6 liner to paint the Queen Anne's lace; keep it airy. From the stem of the flower, add some green lines made with Hauser Medium Green plus Deep Midnight Blue that go into the clusters of the flower. Start to pity-pat this green mix in for your darks. Remember that these are clusters of flowers. Don't take this dark to the top of your clusters. Next pick up Hauser Medium Green, then tip the brush into Light Buttermilk. Loosely pity-pat over where you started, working upward. Your final pity-pat will be Celery Green tipped in Light Buttermilk. When you have achieved the shape you can go back and add more dark, medium or light values and some stronger Titanium White highlights. Shade your stems with Hauser Medium Green plus Deep Midnight Blue. Highlight with Light Buttermilk.

8. Make a circle for the cornflowers. Use a no. 2 liner and pull thick and thin strokes of thinned Deep Midnight Blue out from the center of the circle. Repeat with Country Blue, then Winter Blue and finally with Light Buttermilk. Also add a few strokes of Dioxazine Purple. Paint the stems with Hauser Medium Green plus Deep Midnight Blue.

9. Use a no. 6 round for the daisy. Load your brush with Titanium White and tip in Golden Straw. Pull petal strokes. Shade against the centers of the petals with a float of Sable Brown. Pull Sable Brown lines onto the petals. Paint the daisy centers with Golden Straw. Shade with Sable Brown plus Burgundy Wine. Highlight with Light Buttermilk, then Titanium White. Add dots of Burnt Umber plus Lamp Black around the daisy centers and out onto some petals with the tip of the liner brush.

10. Paint the bow with Winter Blue, shade with Country Blue, then Deep Midnight Blue. Highlight with Light Buttermilk, then Titanium White.

11. When the design is dry, spatter over the surface with thinned Burgundy Wine plus Mocha, and then maybe thinned Burnt Umber.

12. Add the inset lines to both pieces with Winter Blue. Paint the lettering with Country Blue. Varnish.

INSET LINE

ROUTED EDGE

© Bobbie Gray '00

These patterns may be hand-traced or photocopied for personal use only. Enlarge the above pattern at 200% on a photocopier to return to full size.

This pattern is shown full size.

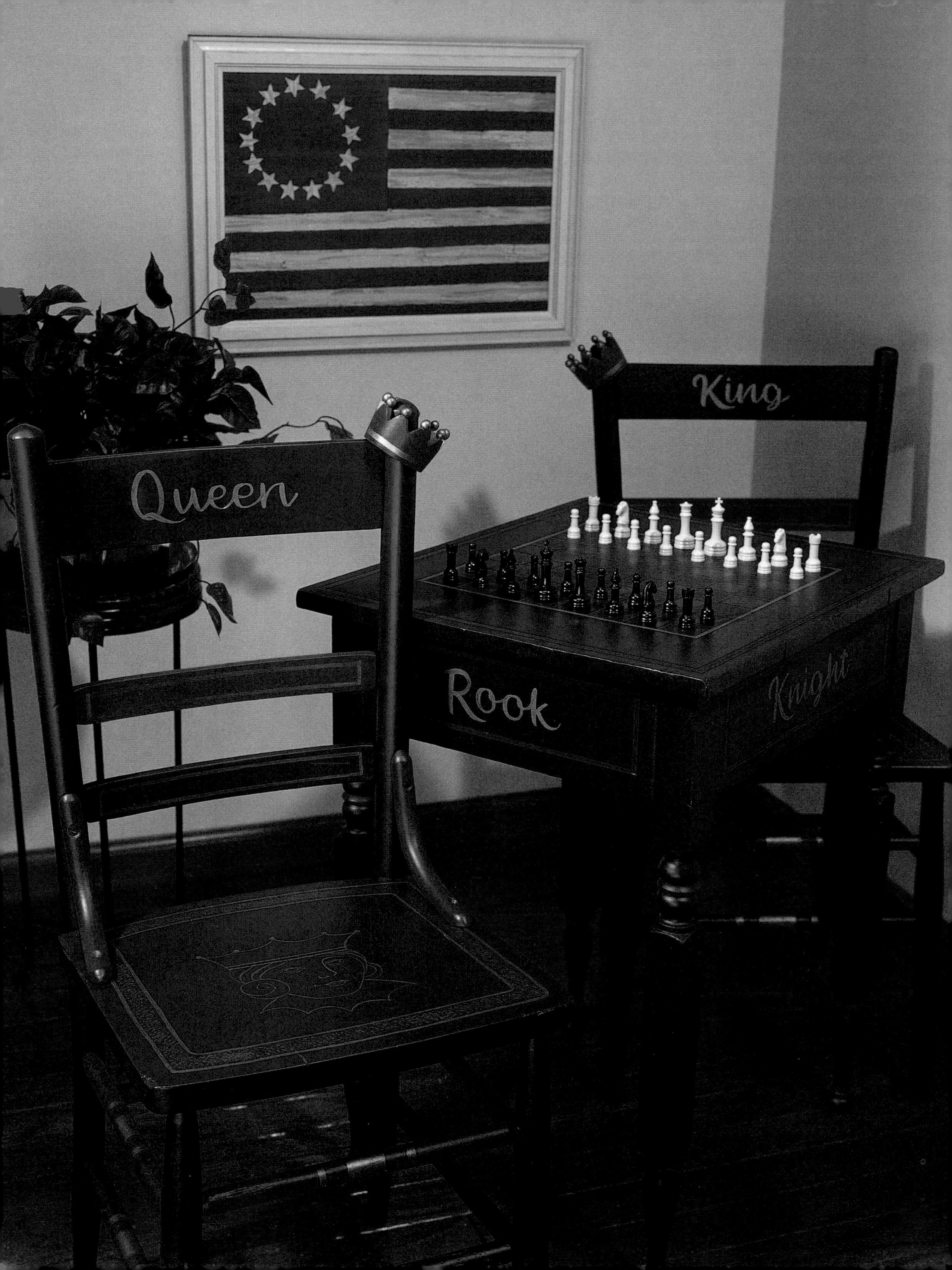
Queen
King
Rook
Knight

Chess Table and Chairs

This project is our pride and joy. Here was an opportunity to take some old flea market finds and make a decorated set that looks good and is useful. This project uses the checkerboard trick from page 79 and illustrates how decorating with words can revive old pieces of furniture. This set should give you some ideas about some of the old pieces around your place.

1. Sand and seal all surfaces.
2. Basecoat the table and chairs with Rustoleum Navy Blue spray paint.
3. Paint the checkerboard by taping off every other line with Magic Tape, then filling the squares with color. We used Country Red. Let dry.
4. Paint the lettering and the outlines on the chair seats with Glorious Gold.
5. Spray varnish was used to protect the entire surface, particularly the tabletop, since it will take more use. You can use your favorite varnish here.
6. Paint the little crowns with Glorious Gold and Country Red.

MATERIALS

DecoArt Americana Acrylic Paints

Country Red DA18	Dazzling Metallics Glorious Gold DA71

Surface
wooden children's table with chairs

Other Supplies
- Rustoleum Navy Blue spray paint
- Magic Tape
- wooden crowns from Zim's (optional)

Hint
Magic Tape is better than cellophane tape because it reduces the puddling effect around the edges, making the lines straight and exact.

This pattern may be hand-traced or photocopied for personal use only. Enlarge at 200% on a photocopier to return to full size.

Glossary

Acrylic Paint
Water-soluble paint used by most decorative artists.

Air Space
Area between letters in a word or around entire copy area.

Bar
Brushstroke width formed by pulling the brush down or across.

Base Line
Bottom line indicating the bottom of all letters that form a word.

Basecoat
Apply two opaque coats of paint to your surface after it has been sanded and sealed. Dry between coats.

Border
Blank area extending to the edge of the surface.

Brushstroke
Weight or width of area formed by pulling the brush through one stroke, also known as a vertical bar or horizontal bar.

Cap Line
Uppermost line indicating the top of capital (uppercase) letters.

Center Line
Line formed horizontally measuring the middle of the height of the uppercase letters.

Connector
Small stroke that connects strokes to form letters or to join lowercase letters, forming words.

Crossbar
Brushstroke formed left to right horizontally as in **E** or **T**.

Descender Line
Line aligning the downstroke distance of lowercase letters.

Downstroke
Vertical brushstroke movement.

Enamel Paint
Paint containing mineral spirits, used mostly for outdoor projects.

Extended Letter
Wide formation of a standard letter.

Foam Core
Two-sided illustration cardstock with foam in the middle.

Horizontal Stroke
Brushstroke pulled from left to right, also known as a crossbar.

Layout
Drawing of proposed copy indicating size and formation of letters.

Linework
Thin your paint to an inky consistency and load on a liner brush by pulling color out from the puddle of paint.

Lowercase Letters
Commonly called small letters, the opposite of capital or uppercase letters.

Mechanical Spacing
Method of placing letters to form words without regard to air space, such as typewriter spacing.

Offset Ruler
Standard ruler with metal strip embedded along one side.

Outline
Unfilled letter drawn, traced or pounced with chalk or charcoal.

Pattern
Proposed copy drawn on paper (tracing or perforated) for transposing to a project.

Parchment Paper
A strong, often somewhat transparent paper that works well with all types of paint.

Perforations
Holes formed in a pattern by pressing a pounce wheel over the paper.

Pity-Pats
Lightly pat up and down in given area with your brush.

Poster Board
Cardstock in large sizes.

Poster Paint
Flat paint containing mineral spirits, commonly used on cardstock.

Pounce Bag
Cloth or sock formed into a small bag and filled with powdered charcoal or chalk. Used to pat powder through perforations to make outlines of letters on a surface.

Pouncing
Act of patting perforated paper pattern with powder in a pounce bag.

Pounce Wheel
Pencil-like tool with a pointed wheel on the end used to perforate a paper pattern.

Script Letters
Letters shaped like handwriting.

Shade
To shade in decorative painting, side load your brush with a deeper value of the base color and float this value in the dark or shadow area.

Slip-Slap
Apply paint in a crisscross pattern with a flat brush. Do this gently.

Spacing
Area between letters or around work copy. Also called air space.

Stylus
Metal, pencil-like tool with a ball end used with transfer paper to transfer patterns to the surface.

Touch-Down Stroke
Touch the tip of your brush down gently, then lift.

Uppercase Letters
Commonly called capital letters.

Vellum
Traditionally, vellum was made from lamb-, kid- or calf-skin. In this book it refers to any transparent, treated paper.

Waistline
The top line of lowercase letters, aptly named because it is waist high, or slightly higher than halfway up an uppercase letter.

Wash
Thin your paint to a transparent consistency, load on brush and apply.

Sayings and Quotations

A baby is a gift from God.

A baby is love, joy and life.

A cat's a cat, and that's that.

A cat's purr is happiness rumbling under its fur.

A clean house is a sign of a misspent life.

A dog is love wagging its tail.

A friend in need is a friend indeed.

A good friend is like a teddy bear.

A good neighbor is a treasure.

A hug a day keeps the blues away.

A little boy is the only thing God can use to make a man.

A new day brings hope.

A new day dawns.

A rainbow is heavenly art.

A son is a dream builder.

After fifty, it's only a matter of maintenance.

All hearts come home for Christmas.

Alleluia, He is risen.

America the Beautiful

Angels Abide

Antique Bears

Antiques for Sale

As for me and my house, we will serve the Lord.

Baby sleeping.

Back door guests are always welcome.

Bah Humbug!

Bath…5 cents

Be an original, not a copy.

Be patient till your wings are grown.

Be someone special, be a teacher.

Bear Collector

Bear Crossing

Bear Necessities

Bear with me.

Bears for Sale

Blarney Spoken Here

Bless the bowlers.

Bless this family.

Bless this food.

Bless this house.

Bless this mess.

Bless this messy kitchen.

Blessed be the children.

Blessed be the golfers.

Blessed be the painters.

Blessed be the quilters.

Bloom where you are planted.

Bottle Collector

Bubble baths…5 cents

Bubble baths given with love.

Bunny Crossing

Call your mother, she worries.

Carpe Diem

Cats adore obedient people.

Cats make life purr-fect.

Chance made us meet, hearts made us friends.

Cherish yesterday, dream tomorrow, live today.

Chocolate is my favorite vegetable.

Chocolate is the answer.

Christmas comes but once a year.

Christmas is love.

Cleanliness is next to Godliness.

Climb to the top of the hill, the sun is shining there.

Country Hay Rides

Creative minds are rarely tidy.

Daisies don't tell.

Dare to dream.

Deadlines amuse me.

Dear Santa—I want it all.

Deer Crossing

Dentists have a lot of pull.

Diet is a four-letter word.

Discover wildlife—have kids.

Do all things with love.

Do not disturb.

Dogs are children who eat on the floor.

Don't drive faster than your guardian angel can fly.

Don't even think of parking here.

East to west, you are the best.

Enjoy life.

Enjoy this day.

Families are forever.

Family provides shelter, roots and wings.

Fishing is the answer; who cares what the question is.

Flower Shoppe

Follow your dream.

Forty isn't old if you're a tree.

Fresh Eggs

Friends are flowers in love's garden.

Friends are for hugging.

Friends are gifts we give ourselves.

Friends are not luxuries, they are necessities.

Friends hear with the heart.

Friends make time for each other.

Friendship is a sheltering tree.

Friendship, like the setting sun, sheds kindly light on everyone.

Friendship multiplies our joy.

Free ride in a police car if you are caught shoplifting.

Frog Crossing

From my lips to God's ears.

Garden Angels

Give thanks for all your blessings.

God bless our home.

God bless this mess.

God blesses the kitchen—but He doesn't clean it.

God made smiles and hugs and granddaughters.

Golfer's diet—live on greens.

Gone fishin'!

Goodnight, sleep tight.

Goodnight, sweetheart.

Grandfathers are great.

Grandmas are for loving.

Grandpas are great.

Grandpas never run out of hugs.

Guardian Angel

Happiness is homemade.

Happy is the home that shelters a friend.

Have yourself a merry little Christmas.

He will give his angels charge over you.

Ho! Ho! Ho!

Ho! Ho! Hum!

Hold on to your dream.

Home is where memories are made.

Home is where the heart is.

Home is where the hug is.

Home sweet apartment

Home sweet home

Homemade Bread

Homemade Cookies

Homemade Pies

Hope springs eternal.

Horse lovers are stable people.

Housework causes warts.

Housework is a bummer.

Hug the chef.

Hunger is the spice of life.

I am uniquely me.

I believe in angels.

I believe in children.

I believe in rainbows.

I believe in Santa.

I believe in the tooth fairy.

I can't bear it without you.

I hate four letter words—wash, iron, dust, cook.

I kiss better than I cook.

I know I can.

I love country.

I was not born to fail.

I'd rather be flying.

I'd rather be golfing.

I'd rather be napping.

If all else fails, ask Grandpa.

If mama's not happy, nobody's happy.

If there is no wind, row.

I'm hooked on fishing.

In every storm there is a patch of blue.

In this house we do not smoke, so keep your butt outside.

Is there life before coffee?

Jesus loves the little children.

Jingle Bells

Jingle for Kringle

Joy!

Joy comes with the morning.

Joyeux Noel

Kindness nourishes the soul.

Kindness strengthens our spirit.

Kiss the cook.

Kwitcherbellyachin

Laughter is sunshine.

Let a smile be your umbrella.

Let it snow.

Let not your heart be afraid.

Let not your heart be troubled.

Let us love one another.

Let us love one an-udder.

Life gives scraps—make quilts.

Life is a game—football serious.

Life is a gift.

Life is full of blessings.

Life is meant to be shared.

Life is precious…handle with prayer.

Life is uncertain—eat dessert first.

Life's most precious gifts are those tied with heartstrings.

Light fades, stars appear, evening angels gather here.

Live and let live.

Live, love and be happy.

Live well…laugh often…love much.

Lord give us patience to endure our blessings.

Love abides here.

Love abides in this home.

Love in the home puts joy in the heart.

Love is a choice.

Love is always in season.

Love is the heart in bloom.

Love is the heart of marriage.

Love, laughter and friends welcome here.

Love one another.

Love will light your way.

Loving hearts make a home.

Maid's Day Off

Marriage: Love is the heart of it.

May all your Christmas dreams come true.

May all your tomorrows be as happy as today.

May Christmas happen in your heart.

May this house, to every guest, be a place of peace and rest.

May your day be as special as you are.

Meals in this kitchen are cooked with love.

Meowy Christmas.

Music—love in search of a word.

My Brother, My Friend

My get-up-and-go got up and went.

My heart belongs to you.

My kitchen and I welcome you.

My other house is cleaner.

My Sister, My Friend

Neighbors are side-by-side friends.

Never play leapfrog with a unicorn.

Noel

No Smoking

Notice: Unattended children will be sold as slaves.

Nurses call the shots.

Nursing is the gentle art of caring.

Oh well! Tomorrow's another day.

Old friends are dearest.

One day at a time.

One good reason for teaching: snow.

Open for Business

Over the speed limit, but still in the race.

Peace be with you.

Peace to all who enter here.

Pick up after yourself.

Please don't eat the daisies.

Please don't hog the bathroom.

Please wipe your feet.

Ponder the path of thy feet.

Praise Be!

Praise Him.

Praise the Lord.

Quilts: Blankets of Love

Rejoice!

Readin', Writin' 'n' 'Rithmetic Taught With Love

Reel men wear aprons.

Reservations—my favorite thing for dinner.

Rise and shine.

Santa Crossing

Santa stops here.

Santa's on his way.

Seasoned With Love

Season's Greetings!

Secretaries are letter perfect.

Self-cleaning kitchen—clean up after yourself.

Shepherd Crossing

Shave and a haircut—2 bits

Shhh—baby sleeping!

Sisters are special.

Sisters are there when you need them.

Snowmen come from heaven unassembled.

So this isn't exactly home sweet home. Adjust.

Some of my best friends are children.

Somebunny loves you.

Spring is a new beginning.

Sun shines where love grows.

Superman lives in our garage.

Take it easy.

Teachers have more class.

Teacher, you are the apple of my eye.

Teenagers are hormones with feet.

Thank heaven for little boys.

Thank heaven for little girls.

Thank you for not smoking.

Thank you, call again.

The best antiques are old friends.

The best place to be is in a loving family.

The best thing to spend on your child is love.

The cat knows who the boss is.

The computer made me do it.

The early bird cooks his own breakfast.

The flower of love never fades.

The Lord is my shepherd.

The Luck of the Irish

The only difference between men and boys is the price of their toys.

The road to the house of a friend is never long.

The spirit of Christmas is love.

The Ten Commandments are NOT multiple choice.

The time to be happy is now.

There are two things to give your children—one is roots, the other wings.

There will never be another me.

There's no friend like a mother.

This is a day the Lord has made, rejoice and be glad in it.

This is a positive-thinking area.

This is a smoke-free environment.

This kitchen self-destructs when I'm tired.

Those who enter must wear a smile.

Thou shalt not bellyache!

Thou shalt not park here!

Thou shalt not whine!

Time spent teaching is never lost.

To teach is to learn twice.

To teach is to touch a life forever.

Today is the first day of the rest of your life.

Together: The nicest place to be.

Time is a treasure.

Time marches on.

Time waits for no man.

Triumph—"umph" added to "try."

Walk in sunshine and in love.

We love country in the city.

Welcome Aboard

Welcome Friends

Welcome to our home.

What teachers write on the chalkboard of life can never be erased.

When friends meet, hearts warm.

When in doubt—worry.

When the going gets tough, the tough go shopping.

Where there's a will, there's a way.

Wildlife Refuge

With age comes wisdom.

Women are meant to be loved, not understood.

Wonder Woman Lives Here

Work is a four-letter word.

Work is for people who don't know how to play golf.

You are loved.

You are one of a kind: perfect.

You are the apple of my eye.

You may touch the dust, but don't write in it.

Resources

3M
Phone: (651) 737-6501
Web site: www.mmm.com
(Scotch Magic Tape)

Creative Xpress
295 W. Center St.
Provo, UT 84601
Phone: (800) 563-8679
Fax: (801) 373-1446
E-mail: sales@creativexpress.com
Web site: www.creativexpress.com
(project 4, CC picket fence)

Custom Wood by Dallas
2204 Martha Hulbert Dr.
Lapeer, MI 48446-8091
Phone: (800) 251-7154
(project 2, lazy Susan)

DecoArt
P.O. Box 327
Stanford, KY 40484
Phone: (606) 365-3193
Fax: (606) 365-9739
E-mail: paint@decoart.com
Web site: www.decoart.com
(Americana acrylic paints)

Fred's Frames and Woodworks
3807 Seiler Rd.
Dorsey, IL 62021
Phone: (618) 377-3200
(surfaces for projects 3, 5, 7, 8 and 9)

Hunt Corporation
Web site: www.hunt-corp.com
(Bienfang 20 lb. white poster layout
paper)

Keysan
P.O. Box 5146
Pittsburgh, PA 15206
Phone: (800) 969-5397
Fax: (888) 834-9090
E-mail: keysan@workstuff.com
Web site: www.keysan.com
(retailer for Sanford Artgum and
Pink Petal erasers)

Michaels Stores, Inc.
P.O. Box 619566
DFW, TX 75261-9566
Phone: (972) 409-1300
Web site: www.michaels.com
(project 1, signboard)

One Shot, LLC
P.O. Box 6369
Gary, IN 46406
Phone: (219) 949-1684
Fax: (219) 949-1612
E-mail: kledbett@netnitco.net
Web site: www.1shot.com
(1-Shot lettering enamels and poster
paints)

*Royal & Langnickel
Brush Mfg.*
6707 Broadway
Merrillville, IN 46410
(Langnickel brushes)

Zim's, Inc.
4370 South 300 West
Salt Lake City, UT 84107-2630
Phone: (801) 268-2505
(wooden crowns for project 11)

Index